New Words and a
Changing American Culture

NEW WORDS

and a

Changing American Culture

Raymond Gozzi, Jr.

University of South Carolina Press

Published in Columbia, South Carolina, by the
University of South Carolina Press.

Manufactured in the United States of America.

*Certain portions of this book contain language which some may find
offensive. The use of such language is neither promoted nor encouraged
by the University of South Carolina. The views expressed herein are to
be attributed to their author and do not necessarily represent those of
the University of South Carolina.*

Library of Congress Cataloging-in-Publication Data

Gozzi, Raymond.
    New words and a changing American culture / Raymond Gozzi, Jr.
       p.   cm.
    Includes bibliographical references.
    ISBN 0-87249-693-7. — ISBN 0-87249-694-5 (pbk.)
    1. English language—United States—Lexicology.   2. English
language—Social aspects—United States.   3. United States-
-Civilization—1970–   4. Words, New—English.   5. Americanisms.
I. Title.
PE2830.G6   1990
423′.0973—dc20   90-34482
                                                                      CIP

To my parents:
Irene Murray Gozzi
Raymond D. Gozzi

CONTENTS

Contents

TABLES

ACKNOWLEDGMENTS

This book started its life as a dissertation and owes much to my doctoral committee in the Communication Department at the University of Massachusetts, Amherst: Dr. Vernon Cronen, Chair, Dr. Alison Alexander, Dr. Jane Blankenship, as well as Dr. Norman Sims of the Journalism Department. Each committee member was extremely helpful and patient with an evolving project.

My family is owed much gratitude for their assistance which came in many forms: Dr. Raymond Gozzi, Sr., the late Irene Murray Gozzi, Elizabeth Gozzi Youngberg, and my wife Barbara Logan.

The project would not have been possible without the expert services of Jean Hebert, typist and word processor. Coding assistance from Maureen Eldredge and Mark Doherty was reliable in many senses. Others who lent their advice on various matters include Dr. Frederick Mish, Dr. Susan Parrish Sprowl, three anonymous reviewers, a copy editor, and Managing Editor Earle Jackson. All shortcomings of this manuscript are, of course, my responsibility. Special thanks are due to Warren Slesinger, an editor at the University of South Carolina Press for his interest and encouragement. Thanks to Bradley University for grants to complete the manuscript.

INTRODUCTION

This book is a study of new words (and new definitions for older words) that have entered the language in the quarter century between 1961 and 1986. It is intended for the general reader, although scholars should find it useful as well. It is not a work of linguistics which focuses primarily on the language itself. Rather, it is a form of cultural study, using an unusual source, a dictionary of new words. Since the source is a dictionary, not every slang term or trendy word of recent coinage will be found. However, this study of new words allows us to discuss changes in the culture as a whole from approximately 1961 to 1986, which is its primary purpose.

The primary source material for this book is a dictionary of new words, *12,000 Words* (1986) produced by Merriam-Webster as a supplement to their *Webster's Third Unabridged Dictionary* (1961). Words from *12,000 Words* are italicized in the text. None of these words were contained in the 1961 *Unabridged*, at least in their current definitions.

It is valuable to set off new words typographically so that we may reflect on the changes they signal. However, lists of new words, by themselves, would be indigestible and unreadable. Therefore I have sorted these words into related categories, and used them to construct narratives about the culture of the 1961 to 1986 period. This technique *contextualizes* the new words, and also allows us to see what stories can be told with them. For each new word is a bit of experience encoded into the language. We can get a sense "in our own words" of the changing experiences of the turbulent 1960s, 1970s, and 1980s.

The first chapter, "Words as Memories," traces the history of the times through its new words. In addition, a content analysis was performed on over half the pages of the dictionary *12,000 Words*. This social science technique shows the different areas of discourse that have contributed new words to the language. It finds, for example, that almost half the new words in the dictionary come from Science and Technology.

The second chapter, "New Additions to the City of Words," uses the metaphor of language as a city, proposed by Wittgenstein (1953), to discuss the findings of the content analysis. A more detailed description of the research procedure is given in Appendix 2, along with a complete table of the results.

Chapters 3 through 8 discuss the new words in more detail, using narratives constructed with the new words to tell stories about the changes in each area. These chapters may be read in any order. The new words map for us changes in all areas of the culture: Science and Technology (Chapter 3), Lifestyles (Chapter 4), Economy and Society (Chapter 5), Types of People and Action (Chapter 6), Communication (Chapter 7), and Psychological States (Chapter 8).

The final chapter discusses the kind of social reality that our new words will help us create in the future. Our cultural study ends with some predictions.

Appendix 1 will be of interest to those with theoretical questions about language, experience, and dictionaries.

Appendix 2 describes the research procedures for conducting the content analysis that structures much of the book. The content analysis of *12,000 Words* included more than half of the entries, leading to a statistically reliable sample. The narratives that constitute the bulk of each chapter, however, are taken from the entire dictionary, and are not limited to words covered in the sample.

New Words and a
Changing American Culture

CHAPTER ONE

Words as Memories

Why Study New Words?

New words are the cutting edge of language. They carve sounds into new shapes and give form to new aspects of experience.

New words are mysterious—anonymous pieces of human creativity. They bubble up through the cultural conversation at unpredictable moments. They begin life as outlaws, unsanctioned by the guardians of cultural propriety. They struggle for acceptance through an inherently democratic process of choice—will they catch on or will they slip into alphabetic oblivion? Will they take the country by storm, only to disappear as quickly as yesterday's news? Or will they quietly take their place in the working vocabulary of the culture, competently encoding some new shard of experience?

New words tend to slip into our conversation without our paying too much attention. Simply recalling and pointing out the new words that have entered the vocabulary between 1961 and 1986 serves a useful purpose—particularly for young people who accept their received vocabulary as a given. New vocabulary can also be interesting for those who have lived through the period studied, as a way to look back and imagine what life was like before we had the word *yuppie*, for example. Somehow, we managed to get along without it, as we did without *microwave ovens, microcomputers,* and *micrographics.*

A new word is a condensed, codified bit of experience. It exists because people have noticed something new. Therefore new words are markers of cultural attention. By studying new words, we can tell where the culture has newly focused its attention, what it has been talking about. New words answer the eternal question: what's new?

For those of us looking back, new words encode memories: what was new, back in the 1960s? The term *Black Power* reminds us of a militant stage of the Civil Rights movement; the term *counterproductive* brings back the techno-jargon of the Vietnam War.

1

This book puts new words together to tell stories, to gain perspectives on the changes of the times. The stories composed of new words highlight changes in the culture's attention. Certainly, older words continue to be used. This study does not measure constancy of language use. Instead it maps the distinctively new areas of experience in the culture during the quarter century from 1961 to 1986.

But a study of new words is more than a stroll down *memory lane*, pleasant though that may be. The new words that have "made it" into *12,000 Words* (Merriam-Webster, 1986) are largely part of the working vocabulary of the culture. They are in use, doing what language does—carving out an interpreted reality, within which we live, think, and act. We think with these new words, we communicate with them, to some extent we follow where their implications lead us.

And so a study of new words becomes a study in prediction. Using this view of language as a reality-constructor, we can ask ourselves just what labels and what interpretations our vocabulary provide us with to face the newness of the future. What is the reality going to be like that we are constructing with our language, and within which we will all live? Those readers mainly interested in cultural predictions are welcome to turn directly to Chapter 9, "Words As Predictors." Chapters may be read in any order. This chapter will use the new words as memories, to trace political and cultural changes in the tumultuous quarter-century between 1961 and 1986.

From Camelot to Postmodernism

We may mark the beginning and ending points of the period from 1961 to 1986 by the two words *Camelot* and *postmodernism*. *Camelot* was the title of a play about Arthurian England, popular in the early 1960s, which became applied to the Kennedy presidency. It came to mean a time of idyllic happiness, with its imagery of pure knights fighting evil for fair maidens.

Postmodernism, the *trendy buzz word* of the late 1980s, by contrast, portrays a consciousness so fragmented as to be schizophrenic, an art so eclectic as to defy categorization, and a language fascinated by self-contradiction and oxymorons. Some critics deny *postmodernism* exists at all, while others have written books on it. Even authors called *postmodern* can't agree on a definition for the term. Somehow the confusion is appropriate, symptomatic of a larger state of affairs in the culture at the end of our period.

Camelot and *postmodernism* highlight a pair of interrelated themes in American culture during our period: the culture became more complex and more contentious.

The increasing complexity of the culture can be seen in a variety of statistics. For example, in the year 1960, 12,000 new books and editions were published. In the year 1983, over 53,000 new books and editions appeared. In 1960 there were 559 television stations, but by 1985 there were 1,206 (from Jeffres, 1986).

The country continued its century-long trend toward urbanization. In 1960, 63 percent of the population resided in metropolitan areas. By 1986, over 76 percent did (U.S. Dept. of Commerce, 1987). The new word *technopolis* was coined to capture the mix of technology and urbanization which produced the automobile-based *urban sprawl*. Other new words tell a story of *politicization* and contentiousness within the new urban and suburban culture.

Politicization in Technopolis

The period saw the *supercity* emerge from *urban sprawl*. *Manhattanization* took place when *high-rises* appeared in the *inner city* through *urban renewal* programs. Rents went up and *gentrification* displaced the *underclass* to other city neighborhoods, which were deserted by *white flight*. *Ticky-tacky tract homes* were hurriedly built in the *slurbs*. Poorer areas got *red-lined* for bank loans, and *white backlash* threatened *resegregation*. The new *metro* regions became increasingly *malapportioned* politically due to the population shifts.

Programs designed to cast a *safety net* under the *underclass* were cyclically increased and then *defanged*, accused of being *creeping socialism*. Welfare was pressured to become *workfare*. Food stamps and *AFDC* (aid to families with dependent children) programs became political footballs. *Medicare* faced constant opposition. There was a shortage of *day-care centers*. *Halfway houses* and *crisis centers* appeared in most cities, as the problems of the *broken home* received public attention.

Clearly, the benefits of *technopolis* did not extend to all. Efforts by *minorities* to be included were often met by *tokenism*, finding a *house nigger* or *Uncle Tom* to satisfy appearances. In the struggle to integrate schools, *pro-bussing* advocates often met with *white backlash*.

The Civil Rights struggle in the South, with its *Freedom Rides* and *sit-ins*, gave blacks a pride in *blackness*, and a sense of identity as *soul brothers* and *sisters*. *Black Studies* were added to the curricula of many schools, and *Black English* was recognized as a legitimate dialect. Groups like the *Black Panthers* and *black nationalists* generally sought to promote an agenda of *black power*. Old-style "negroes" were derided as *accommodationists*.

Other *minority* or oppressed groups became active as well. Spanish-Americans developed their own *ethnic* pride called *Chicanismo*, after the words *chicano* and *chicana*. Many homosexuals *came out* of the *closet* and marched in the streets for *gay liberation*. *Women's liberation* called for the *sisterhood* of all women and the ending of *sexism* in a male–*chauvinist* society. And with the *graying* of the population, militant *Gray Panthers* sought an end to *ageism*.

These movements of protest were loosely joined together in the public mind into a *counterculture*. This agglomeration of people was generally *anti-authoritarian*, *anti-nuke*, *anti-war*, and against technology that was *anti-human*. Its ranks included students of the *New Left*, *hippies*, *Flower People*, *minorities*, and even wealthy *limousine liberals* being *radical chic*. It is possible that such a diverse group never really existed as an entity, except as an extension of the entertainment industries, who sold them rock music and blue jeans. Was the *counterculture* merely a fad, *co-opted* by clever *establishment* forces into *pop culture* posturings and away from meaningful social change? For affirmative views on this question, see Martin (1981) and Gitlin (1980).

Or was the *counterculture* a term for a still-crystallizing response to an overdependence on technology, and an attempt at *greening* (rejuvenating) different aspects of social life? The author tends to side with this latter interpretation.

In any case the diversity of goals and programs, and the elusiveness of the enemies in the *establishment*, meant that it was extremely difficult to tell when one was *copping out*, being *co-opted* into the *mainstream* culture. The more repressive aspects of *Amerika* were obvious, but the subtler repressions of *the system* required careful scrutiny. Many people turned to different forms of *consciousness-raising*, hoping for *demystification* of their life situation. Would there be a *greening* of America? Could *the system* be reformed from within, by *incrementalism*? Or were such ideas merely leading to *complicity* in the injustices of *the system*?

While remnants of the *New Left* agonized over such issues, the 1980s produced a vocal *New Right*, which formed around issues like abortion and religion. *Neoconservatives* were *anti-radical, anti-black, anti-feminist, anti-obscenity*, and against what they saw as the excesses of the *counterculture* in general. *Pro-life* advocates battled *pro-choice* people verbally and sometimes physically. *Birchers* and *survivalists* insisted a nuclear war could be fought and won. *Hawks* and other *hardliners* opposed *doves* and *peaceniks* about Vietnam and nuclear weapons. *Born-again* Christians became politically active and "televangelists" became visible on *the tube* as they sought a return to traditional standards of morality.

Thus the landscape of *technopolis* became heavily politicized. As is usual in mass cultures, only a minority was active at any time, while the majority was relatively passive—leading to claims that different *spokespeople* really spoke for the "silent majority."

Postmodern or Hyper-Modern?

Many names have been suggested for the new society that was seen emerging between 1961 and 1986. *Technetronic* society (shaped by advances in technology and communications), *cyberculture* (served by cybernated industry), the information society, a service economy, a media society, are all terms which capture some aspects of the changes.

A suggestion by Bell (1973), the *postindustrial* society, has been taken up with rather more enthusiasm than the author himself wished. Bell claims that *postindustrial* society has not yet arrived, while others picked up the term and applied it to our period. There has been a trend toward employment in the service and information sectors of the economy over the quarter century, and a society that produces information is vastly different from one that produces hardware.

The term *postmodern* has come into increasing use, particularly in cultural studies of various sorts. Different authors give different definitions of the term (see Foster, 1983). *12,000 Words* defines it as: "of or relating to any of several artistic movements that are reactions against the philosophy and practices of modern arts or literature."

Postmodernism as a term started in architecture, where it covers various departures from the plain geometric styles of modernism. In literature, the term came to be applied to a varied group of writers, who, if they had anything in common, showed a concern for style over substance, for the play of words and the paradoxes of experience. In visual arts, *postmodernism* meant an accent on surfaces and reflection. Eclectic pastiche replaced consistent styles in all art forms.

An influential critical *postmodernism* came to be associated with practices of *deconstruction*, with its heavy focus on language. Psychological *postmodernism* focused on the theories of French psychiatrist Jacques Lacan, who proposed understanding the unconscious mind in linguistic terms. The mind-set of *postmodernism*, with its fragmented attention, was compared to schizophrenia (Jameson, 1983).

As an umbrella term, *postmodernism* has captured many of the unique changes in aesthetic experience of our period. This author disagrees that we are in a *post*modern era. Rather, all the qualities which come under this rubric imply a "hyper-modern" era.

We have not experienced the end of modern society, but its triumph. We are living in modernism in high gear. The frantic rush for the new, the "modern," now has more outlets, more avenues, more consumer goods; but it is the same engine that has driven modernism since English cotton mills started turning out mass-produced fashions in the 1700s.

Just because painters are not necessarily painting in a way once called "modernism" does not mean that the underlying impulse of modernism—incessant change and search for the new—has vanished. *Postmodern* works of art are just modernism in its newest fad, its newest clothes, the better to sell itself.

For that is the underlying fact that has not changed. Selling, money, wealth, are still the determinants of success, both in the art world and the rest of the society. They determine success because they are the fundamental forms of social exchange in the "modern" industrial world. The big cities of the "modern" world remain with us, the big corporate enterprises remain, the big government bureaucracies produced by "modern" "rationalization" remain. It is a trick of the language to call our present society "post" all of this. This is but one of many such tricks of language in our period. How do we study such a "hyper-modern" culture? How do we get a handle on it, if we cannot even agree on a name for it?

Obviously, this culture needs to be studied in many different ways to be comprehended. The approach here is unique, but is only one of many methods. By focusing on the new words generated in this period, we can gain a more *in-depth* story of the changes that have rushed so quickly by.

CHAPTER TWO

New Additions to the City of Words

The Metaphor of the City

In a famous passage the philosopher Wittgenstein (1953, p. 8) compared language to a city. He had in mind an old European city, a maze of little streets and squares, old and new houses crowded together, and buildings with additions from various periods. But he saw clearly the new additions on the outskirts, the scientific terminology which formed straight, regular streets with uniform houses out in the suburbs of the language.

Wittgenstein never elaborated on his metaphor, making it one of the most famous offhand remarks in language studies. The metaphor of language as a city is, of course, a subspecies of the larger metaphor of language as a map, which has been commonly used (see Hayakawa, 1939). In this chapter, the metaphor will be further modified. We will speak of a city of words, rather than of language as a whole. This eliminates troublesome questions about how syntax and grammar fit into the city metaphor. And since new words are our focus here, the city–of–words metaphor allows us to take a comprehensive view of the changes in vocabulary during the period from 1961 to 1986.

Our language lies spread about us like a vast, teeming city. Sometimes we want to see what our city looks like as a whole, so we travel to a nearby hill, or mountain, or fly over in an airplane to see the view.

The city of words, however, is a little more abstract and difficult to observe. Where do we find a hill outside of it, from which to observe it? How can we leave the city of words, especially if we wish to write about it? Any book about words such as this one must come from within a city of words, as well as partly attempt to step outside it. There are, we must remember, many "cities" of many different families of words.

Our technique for observing the city of words in this book, will be the use of the dictionary, *12,000 Words*. The "map" of changes in the city will be drawn with the assistance of a content analysis of the dictionary.

Many metaphorical parallels exist between the physical cities in which we live and the city of words. Certainly the first parallel is that the city of words has suffered from *urban sprawl*, just as its physical counterparts have. According to the editor of the *Oxford English Dictionary*, during the 1961–1986 period, the English vocabulary expanded faster than at any other time in its history, and most of the impetus for the expansion came from the United States (Burchfield, 1986).

In the real city and in the city of words we have problems of *noise*: as *noise pollution* from traffic or as *noise* in the communication sense of meaningless or irrelevant output (here we have a new definition for an obviously older word).

Physical *smog* (a photochemical haze) might be paralleled by verbal *doublespeak*, (a sort of verbal haze), perhaps caused by *bureaucratese, computerese,* or *educationese.*

Difficulty in reception of electronic signals is paralleled by *static* (opposition or criticism) in relationships.

One wonders if the problems of *gridlock*, where traffic congestion forestalls all possible movement, also spill over into the *postmodern* city of words, with its conceptual *gridlock* expressed as oxymorons: "aggressively neutral," "dissonant unity," "unfinished whole."

We can view a dictionary as a census of the city of words, and lexicographers as the census takers. For a word to get included in the dictionary-census, it needs to have been used over a period of time by more than one source. Usually the word must have found its way into print—meaning that words of the *underclasses*, or *minorities*, will probably be underrepresented in the dictionary, even as the people in those categories are often missed in the national census.

Still, during our period, many words from formerly unrecognized sources and subcultures found their way into the cultural conversation, into print, and into the dictionaries.

The dictionary of new words, *12,000 Words* (Merriam-Webster, 1986), which forms the basis for this study, is like a census of new additions to the city of words. It is intended as a general-purpose dictionary, for a wide audience, and provides as good a sampling of newcomers to the city of words as we are likely to find at this close a vantage point. Of course the makeup of the city of words is always changing, and no census is completely accurate. But for a broad overview, which we are taking in this chapter, the dictionary of new words provides an invaluable source.

To get a more detailed picture of the changes in the city of words, the author and two assistants performed a content analysis of the dictionary *12,000 Words*.

More detailed information about the content analysis can be found in Appendix 2. In brief, two assistants were hired and trained in the use of a category system. The object was to code each definition of each word into a category, to determine from what discourse it came. Working independently, the coders agreed on 78.446 percent of their codings (Scott's pi=.7733). This is quite good intercoder agreement, considering that 47 categories were used.

The dictionary has 212 pages. One hundred and sixteen pages were coded, or 54.7 percent of all the pages. The sample size was large enough to expect a margin of sampling error of +/− 1.58 percent (Babbie, 1982).

We will discuss the results of this sampling of the city of words in the next section.

A Tour Through the City of Words

We will begin our tour in the suburbs, because the most dramatic growth in the city of words comes in the scientific suburbs. As a region, Science & Technology terms constitute 45 percent of the new words in *12,000 Words*. (See Table 1.)

This growth of the scientific suburbs reveals a culture preoccupied with technology. The culture is quick to see a technological *fix* for its problems, but often *ripple effects* appear which are unforeseen and put the applications of the technology into question. This leads to a search for yet another technological *fix*, and a self-perpetuating logic places the society squarely into a "techno-trap"—of being dependent upon a technology yet not understanding it or being able to predict its effects. This situation will be discussed at greater length in Chapter 3.

The second most fertile source of new words was the category Lifestyles, with 24 percent of the total. This was the era of the suburban *shopping mall*, in which affluence produced more consumer goods and more alternatives in ways to eat, travel, vacation, work, and go to school. This variety in lifestyles extended

Table 1. *REGIONAL GROWTH IN THE CITY OF WORDS*

Grouping	Number of Words	Percentage of Words
Science and technology	2419	45.235
Lifestyles	1294	24.190
Social-economic terms	611	11.424
Other	455	8.509
People and action	378	7.068
Communication and psychology	190	3.551

to the emergence above ground of formerly underground subcultures of sex and drugs. We see the jargon of city subcultures of sex, drugs, and rock'n'roll invading the suburbs. Addiction becomes a metaphor for much experience in the consumer society, as people speak of being *junk food junkies,* hooked on an author, or *turned on* by a movie. These issues are discussed in Chapter 4.

Yet this variety in lifestyles produced strains and *politicization* throughout the society. We find conflict throughout the city, especially on the borders between the suburbs and downtown. Some of these terms have already been covered in the earlier section of Chapter 1 on "*Politicization* in *Technopolis.*" Intolerance of the most flagrant lifestyle differences led to a resurgence of ideologies in an age when ideology had supposedly ended.

We get downtown with the Social-Economic terms, which provided 11 percent of the new words. Here we see that the economy has become more confusing, unpredictable, *counterintuitive.* As the stakes of a world economy have gotten bigger, the strategies have become less clear. As a result, a vocabulary of game-playing and the *bottom line* have emerged to conceptualize and justify managerial decision making. Sport terms became managerial metaphors as people wondered if the economy could be controlled at all. Social and Economic terms are covered in Chapter 5.

People and Actions made up 7 percent of the new words, and here we find a large crop of terms of denunciation, stereotyping, and ridicule appearing like ugly weeds in vacant lots. This vocabulary is discussed in Chapter 6.

Finally, Communication and Psychology terms provided 3.5 percent of the new words. In the fragmented and contentious social environment, we find a vocabulary emerging quite concerned about *doublespeak, mystification,* and loss of a coherent identity. A continuous inner self became harder to maintain. Instead, energy went into maintaining self-control and managing the performances of the moment. Anxiety became a constant, free-floating problem which resembled stage fright. Relationships suffered as well. Chapters 7 and 8 deal with these areas.

There is an "Other" category containing 8.5 percent of the new words. This reminds us that any category system will miss certain information, and that language as a whole is more complex than its parts can put into words.

Overall, this view of the city of words presents a picture we might label as ironic. The culture achieves great technological power but somehow loses control over its lifestyles. It produces affluence, but also division and strife. It expands into space, but loses sight of its own identity. It produces tremendous military power, but has less security.

One wonders if we haven't passed a cultural point of diminishing returns, where more is less, where "better" is worse. If the new words of the period are any guide, the city of words in 1986 was a less happy and *together* place than it was in 1961.

CHAPTER THREE

The Scientific Suburbs of the City of Words

Rapid Growth of High-Tech Language

The most striking growth in the city of words during our quarter century (1961–1986) comes in the scientific suburbs. As a region, Science & Technology terms constituted 45 percent of the new words in *12,000 Words*. (See Table 2.)

The big story in the scientific suburbs was the growth in terms from "Biology and Chemistry," as the two fields grew closer together in subject matter and vocabulary. Almost 13 percent of the total growth comes from this area.

The second-most growth came in the category of "Scientific and Technical Theory, Math" which produced 8.6 percent of the new words. These top categories together accounted for one in five of all the new words in the dictionary.

The scientific suburbs saw a heavy expansion of their medical sectors, as the category "Medical, Physiology" came in fourth overall, with 6 percent of the new words. "General Technological Terms" accounted for 4 percent, and "Computers" for 3 percent of the new words. The "Pharmaceuticals" sector accounted for 2.8 percent of the new words.

These sectors of the scientific suburbs alone account for over one-third of all the new words in the city of words during the 1961–1986 period.

Terms from "Space," "A-Bombs, Plants, Radiation," and the "Military" accounted for 3.7 percent more. "General Physiology Terms" produced 1.5 percent. And, at the bottom of the list in the scientific suburbs, we find terms from "Environmentalism."

Most of the new terms from Science and Technology are unintelligible to the layperson. This in itself reflects the increased specialization of knowledge in our society, and the widening gap between the knowledge available and the knowledge actually used

Table 2. *SCIENCE AND TECHNOLOGY TERMS*

Overall Rank	No. Words	Category	% Words
1	695	Biology and Chemistry	12.997
2	463	Science and Tech Theory, Mathematics	8.659
4	338	Medical, Physiology	6.321
6	224	General Technological Terms	4.189
10	187	Computers	3.497
12	154	Pharmaceuticals	2.880
14	105	Space	1.963
18	81	Physiology—General	1.514
20	60	A-Bombs, Plants, Radiation	1.122
22	49	Electric Power, Electronics	0.916
27	35	Military	0.654
30	28	Environmentalism	0.523
TOTAL	2419		45.235

by the ordinary citizen. Only when some exceptional situation or crisis occurs does the arcane terminology of science and technology enter the public domain. Take, for example, the new term *retrovirus*, first appearing in *12,000 Words*: "Any of a group of RNA-containing viruses (as the Rous sarcoma virus and the HTLV causing AIDS) that produce reverse transcriptase by means of which DNA is formed using their RNA as a template and incorporated into the genome of infected cells and that include numerous viruses causing tumors in animals including man." If this term were not associated with *AIDS*, it would not be heard outside of specialized contexts.

Obviously, a complete list of scientific and technological terms would be unilluminating and uninformative. More productive will be the selection of certain terms that tell a story—a story about changes in experience in this period. Other stories can certainly be constructed from these terms, but this will be a start.

The main themes of this story are: the increasing complexity of technology, pushing it outside the domain of understanding of most people, combined with an increasing dependence on technology. This dependence upon something not well understood we may call the "techno-trap." In addition, the complex science and technology have effects that are not well understood—that go beyond what was "intended." These "unintended effects" become more pervasive in our period.

The Techno-Trap

As technology has become more pervasive it has become more complex, and therefore less knowable even as we need it more. Much electronic technology has literally retreated inside *black boxes,* where complex circuits are imprinted into *solid-state* circuitry on *microchips.* The resulting "concealed complexity" (Winner, 1977) makes understanding technology even more impossible for the average user.

This situation of simultaneous dependence upon and ignorance of technology is an aspect of the "techno-trap." Some parts of this "trap" are quite comfortable, as the technologies do what they are supposed to; but other parts of the "trap" can become deadly as unforeseen "second-order effects" (Bauer, 1969) appear. Individuals and society as a whole have been caught in a dialectic between "primary, intended effects" and "second-order effects" of technology. In practice, it may not be possible to separate these "effects" (as contended by Ellul, 1964). Debates over new technologies routinely take the form of guesses over "second-order" effects, their magnitudes, *maximum likelihood* of malfunctions, and *acceptable* risks. Those who do not wish to live in the shadow of what the *technostructure* deems to be *acceptable* risks are stigmatized as *luddites.*

The original impetus for much of the Post-World War II technology came from military applications—from the computer to the *microchip.* As warfare became more technologized, and as *smart missiles* and long-range radar were hooked to computer networks, the amount of time for decision-making in major crises was cut down to a few minutes, sometimes only seconds. Despite *fail-safe* designs, it became increasingly necessary to automate the decision-making process, and therefore more difficult to *abort* any decision made. Thus we have the ironic result that a system designed to increase national security actually makes that security more tenuous in some cases.

This dialectic between intended effects and unintended effects underlies the history of technology in our period. Unfortunately, even the most sophisticated *systems theory* has not allowed adequate computer *simulation* of technological effects. In response to crises brought on by unintended "second-order" effects, we seek a *quick fix* from another technology. Such logic self-perpetuates the "techno-trap."

Stalled Technologies

Technological change is not inevitable, nor does it occur in a social vacuum. A group of new words tell a story of *aborted* technological change, change which did not fit in with existing institutional arrangements. Winston (1986) even proposes a "law" (the quotation marks are his) which states that existing institutions act to suppress the radical potentials of technological change.

We can see this "law" in operation in the history of *gasohol*. This blending of gasoline (90 percent) and ethyl alcohol (10 percent) was going to expand the nation's gas supplies by using abundant corn on farms. However, changes in the price of oil caused the abandonment of most gasohol projects, as companies sought to maximize profits in the short run. The long-term need for alternative fuels couldn't show enough short-term profit.

A similar fate befell *cogeneration* plants (harnessing heat generated as a by-product in other processes), *wind turbines, solar panels*, and *solar sails*. These technologies, dubbed "appropriate technologies" by E. F. Schumacher (1973), were not as profitable in the short run as other more *high-tech* products, and perhaps they threatened existing interests too directly. As a result, they were pushed to the margins of economic existence.

Another technological device surrounded by controversy was the *air bag*, for passenger safety in car crashes. Promoted by consumer advocate Ralph Nader as having the potential to save thousands of lives per year, it was resisted by the car manufacturers on various grounds. The technology lay unused for over 20 years.

A final example of technological change needing to accommodate to existing institutional arrangements is the *green revolution*. This was going to eliminate world hunger by supplying *Third World* farmers with pesticides like *dioxin*, along with fertilizers, tractors, and other *high-tech* products. Yet the vast majority of *Third World* farmers could not afford the technology, understand its proper uses, or cope with the skills involved. The materials were bought by rich farmers, who thereby became richer. Instead of eliminating hunger, the *green revolution* increased divisions between rich and poor.

These terms and their accompanying stories illustrate the fact that technological change had to accommodate to institutional pressures, both in this country and abroad. In the United States, the paradoxical result was that the period saw great technological change, but not much change in the composition of the top income brackets or largest corporations (Domhoff, 1983).

Second-Order Effects

In the post-World War II period, new technologies often furthered the *convenience*-oriented *throwaway* consumer culture. The number of electrical gadgets proliferated, from electric toothbrushes to *cordless* telephones, and new plastic items could be fashioned seemingly at will, giving us the extended sense of the term *plastic* as meaning anything not genuine or sincere.

This consumer technology resulted from the control of technological change toward the ends of profit-seeking consumer industries; and furthered the "American life-style" which became such an important justification for corporate capitalism. Yet it also used a very high percentage of the planet's resources, many of them not replaceable. The increasing awareness of the inherent wastefulness of the technologically enhanced consumer lifestyle led to further consideration of "second-order" effects. An incipient ecological awareness was articulated by *environmentalists* seeking to avoid *ecocatastrophe* through consideration of the *bioenvironmental* effects of technology.

Over all the *high-tech* devices fell the shadow of the *Big C*—cancer. The convenience culture embraced *microwave ovens*, yet this new technology had to carry warning labels about leaking radiation. In the 1960s, thousands of color televisions had to be recalled due to "excessive" levels of radiation. And in the 1980s, there were questions about the new *microcomputers* and radiation as well.

Radiation is *tumorigenic*, and also produces *birth defects*. Was the environment becoming more toxic? Was it safe to bathe the public in microwaves from broadcasting, satellites, TVs, computers, ovens? Disturbing evidence of toxic effects was often labeled *anti-science*, and was sometimes suppressed by industry and government (Brodeur, 1977).

Even the technology of medicine, which advanced much during the period, was not free from the dialectic of intended versus unintended effects. Advances in lifesaving resulted from *CPR* (cardiopulmonary resuscitation) techniques and *life-support systems*. Yet these often produced catastrophic costs for families, with no real cures for seriously ill patients, leading to court cases over the right to "pull the plug."

The very line between living and non-living beings—always fuzzy—became even more problematic as *bioelectronic* technologies fashioned *cyborgs*: people hooked into *life-support systems*. *Bionic* organs (mechanical replacements) and organ transplants applied a technology of replaceable parts to humans. While these undoubtedly prolonged life in some cases, they made it harder to tell life from death and people from machines, a theme we will return to in Chapter 9.

Genetic engineers began tinkering with the *gene pool* of different organisms. As outdoor testing of genetically altered bacteria began in the 1980s, the second-order effects could only be guessed at.

Cell irregularities became better understood through *cytotechnology*, yet the *Big C* resisted explanation. The *immune system* received close study, but new diseases such as *Legionnaires' Disease* and *AIDS* posed frightening new threats.

Heralded in the 1960s as a morally liberating technology, or vilified as a destroyer of morals, *the pill*, along with other birth control technologies such as the *morning-after pill* and the *intrauterine device* (*IUD*), allowed unguarded sexual contact. In the 1980s, however, the *retrovirus* which caused *AIDS* threatened to turn the sex-tease culture into a death trap.

This survey of terms for technological change is by no means complete, for, as indicated earlier, most of the terms from science and technology are highly specialized. This section and the next ones, on atomic technologies, *aerospace*, computers, and theoretical terms, give, however, a fair map of the most common technological terms.

Reading through them, one is reminded of how problematic technological change has been in our period, and how much faith must be invested in technologies that we do not understand. Here we find a further irony, that science and technology, which originated in an attack on faith, should now require faith since they have gone beyond the capacity of reason to explain them or predict their effects.

Computers

The word "computer" is very old, and until World War II, meant "a person who computes." Now it refers almost exclusively to machines, either big *mainframes* or the smaller *microcomputers* and *minicomputers*.

The smaller instruments were made possible by the technologies of *microelectronics*, the printing of *integrated circuits* on *microchips* which could serve as *microprocessors*. Such *solid-state* technology allowed the smaller machines to increase their *memory* by many *kilobits* and *kilobytes*.

A *bit* is the basic unit of information in a digital computer—either the presence or absence of a hole, electric current, or magnetized spot. A *byte* is a collection of *bits*. As *memories* and processing capacities grew, thousands of *bytes* were represented in *K* units (two to the 10th power, or 1024 *bytes*), and then millions as *megabits* and *megabytes* (two to the 20th power), and even *gigabits* (one billion *bits*).

As *memories* grew, microprocessors relied on advances in *Random Access Memory (RAM)* and *Read Only Memory (ROM)* circuits, which were soon miniaturized into *microchips*.

Because more areas in the economy are becoming *computerized*, there has been a steady attempt to make them more user-*friendly* (a new definition of the word "friendly," meaning easy for a nonspecialist to use or understand). No longer are computers esoteric machines, understood only by *hackers* and other *computerites* speaking *computerese*. Instead, ordinary office workers must be able to cope with *word processing, modems, local area networks, printouts*, and *electronic mail*. Workers must become familiar with *input* procedures, and must be prepared to have their *keystrokes monitored* by the computer to check on their efficiency. *Work stations* must be *on-line* for a maximum amount of time. *Downtime* must be minimized.

While this situation has the potential for creating mechanized drudgery in the office, as the computer *monitors* each worker, it also has the potential for freeing people from office work by *telecommuting*. If the office can be *accessed* from *remote terminals* in a *network*, then *teleprocessing* will allow *access* to the same *databases* and *data banks* without the need to travel to work.

As part of the attempt to make computers more *friendly*, words from everyday experience are applied to them with new, computer-specific definitions. They are often referred to as *brains*, and advanced applications are called *artificial intelligence*. Data storage capacity becomes *memory*. *Input* of *characters* on a *keyboard* becomes *conversation*. Computers *read* the programming *words* (a combination of electrical or magnetic impulses), and *look them up* (look up function) in an internal *dictionary* (an internally stored list). The computer can then *add, sort, stack, difference* (subtract), *multiply, queue* instructions or operations, *jump* to *subprograms, interrupt* itself, or otherwise *monitor* itself. After it has finished its *computation*, usually in microseconds, it can *display* its results either as a *readout* or as *hard copy* in a *print out*.

Some programs are designed to be *interactive*, providing *friendly* questions to users. Examples include "expert systems," essentially codified knowledge of human experts in specialized fields like medicine or geology. Through a series of *branches* and *loops* the system can apply its *artificial intelligence* to specific problems and produce "judgments."

Of course, even *intelligent* terminals can't judge whether they're being fed *garbage* or not—and *GIGO*: *Garbage In, Garbage Out*. The implications of these human terms for computers will be discussed in Chapter 9.

Still, despite all attempts to make them *friendly*, both *hardware* and *software* have their own *programs, commands, sub-programs*, and *languages*, and codes. *Machine languages* and codes such as *ALGOL* (algorithmic language), *ASCII* (American Standard Code for Information Interchange), *EBCDIC* (Extended Binary Coded Decimal Interchange Code), and *BAL* (Basic Assembly Language) are mainly understood by *computerites*. But programming languages like *BASIC* (Beginner's All-Purpose Symbolic Instruction Code), *LOGO*, and *Pascal* reach wider audiences and are taught in colleges and high schools.

Computers are spreading out into the economy, as purchases can be registered by *bar codes*, and bank transactions can be handled by *EFT* (Electronic Funds Transfer). There are even plans to use computers to replace all cash, and to link the nation's economy into a network of *supercomputers*, into a "cashless, checkless economy."

Computers are entering teaching with *Computer Aided Instruction* (*CAI*) systems and the world of design with *Computer Aided Manufacturing* (*CAM*) systems. The linkage of computers and manufacturing is producing the new science of *robotics*, which could create a *cyberculture* of automated factories and offices.

Besides the capacity for *information processing* which the computer-aided systems bring, they will also have increased ability to *model* different situations, run *simulations* of alternative *scenarios*, and provide increased information.

The second-order effects of a *cyberculture* can only be guessed at. They are clearly of a tremendous magnitude. With *robots* replacing workers and *cybernation* replacing managers, we have the specter of technological unemployment on a grand scale; along with the increased centralization of information and control afforded by a *computerized* economic system.

Space

The exploration of space had begun in literature long before it occurred in fact. Thus, in the 1949 *Webster's New Collegiate Dictionary* (6th Edition), we find the word "space ship"; and in the 7th Edition published in 1963, the words "spaceport" and "space station." Still, Americans found themselves faced with *future shock* when the Russians launched the first orbital satellite in 1957, and the United States Vanguard rocket crashed in flames on its launching pad.

The United States launched a massive effort in the 1960s to get to the moon. New sciences· of *astrobiology, astrochemistry,* and *astrogeology* were developed. The *prelaunch* countdowns received nationwide coverage, and the nation learned the vocabulary of *payloads, birds* (satellites) in *parking orbits, deboosting* (slowing down) and *despinning* spacecraft. The phrase *A-OK* spread across the country in one day after an astronaut used it on a televised launch (Algeo, 1980).

Moon shots with *moon ships* and astronauts taking *moon walks* and watching *earthrise* from the moon occupied the American imagination in the late 1960s and 1970s. Yet then the issue of second-order effects intruded on the dream, and an ironic attitude toward these achievements appeared in the widely used phrase: "if we can put a man on the moon, why can't we . . . ." (provide health care, housing for all, etc. back on earth). (See Newman, 1974.)

Closer to earth, *Comsats* (communications satellites) were developed, and *parked* in *geostationary* or *synchronous* orbits. Satellites could broadcast radio, television, telephone, and digital data over long distances, and could scan the earth for resources or military information through *remote* sensing devices.

These capacities could clearly have second-order effects, as Direct Broadcasting Satellites threatened to take control over the airwaves away from national governments, and *remote* sensing gave satellite owners access to information about any nation's crops, natural resources, troop movements, and natural disasters.

Were *Comsats* providing the infrastructure for some future supranational authority, as they eroded the powers of national governments? Or would they remain as tools in the contest between the superpowers, committed to nationalistic and military ends? By the late 1980s these second-order effects were by no means predictable.

The "Miracle" of the Atom

The biggest "miracle technology" of the Second World War was atomic technology, which produced *the bomb*. Scientists and industry issued utopian predictions for the future of this new energy harnessed for peaceful ends (for a catalog see Del Sesto, 1986). Atomic power plants would make electricity "too cheap to meter," a particularly ironic claim in the 1970s and 1980s when cost overruns of nuclear power plant construction and operation drove utility bills up and pushed some utility owners near bankruptcy. Only gradually did the public learn of the possibility of a *meltdown*, which might produce the *China Syndrome* where the superheated reactor core would melt into the earth. While the industry assured the public the risks were *acceptable*, the question of *fallout* and *post-irradiation* effects on plant and animal life caused serious concern. And the problem of nuclear wastes grew with each year, still seeking a technological *fix*.

There were also promises of nuclear-powered planes (over a billion dollars was spent trying to develop one), nuclear automobiles, and nuclear rockets. Some nuclear power did get into space as power packs for satellites. These posed new problems of nuclear waste, however, when the satellite orbit decayed and the junk reentered the atmosphere.

Radioisotopes found their way into the new medical area of *radiopharmaceuticals*. Bandages and even food were *radio-sterilized*.

But it was *the bomb*, in all its manifestations, which produced the most controversy. It could produce *megadeaths* with one *payload*, but some wondered if it wasn't *overkill*. As missiles got faster, and *payloads* more efficient, they could *deliver* a better *kill ratio*. One missile could be *MIRV'*d to attack several targets simultaneously. Even missiles in *hardened* silos were not safe, so much effort went into developing an *ABM*, or *anti-ballistic missile*.

Yet the *fallout* from the *bomb* could threaten the existence of all life on the planet, as the *radioresistance* of living systems was uncertain, and since radiation could cause unforeseeable mutations in the *gene pool*. This made it questionable whether a nuclear war could be "won" by any side, and led to calls to *denuclearize* certain areas.

In fact, it would not take a war to produce serious *fallout*, nuclear testing itself produced *fallout*, leading to constant pressures for and against *test bans*.

There were also calls to rely more on *conventional* weaponry, to somehow escape the "bomb logic" that seemed to hold the world in its grip.

Yet not many terms from the conventional military arsenal entered the Merriam-Webster sources in this period (more appear in Mager and Mager, 1982). The Vietnam trauma contributed *grunt* (foot soldier) and *frag* (to deliberately attack one's leader with a fragmentation grenade), *Agent Orange*, *free-fire zone*, and *DMZ* (demilitarized zone). The use of *choppers* in *counterinsurgency* actions became widespread throughout the world, as *fire fights* required swift movement of troops. *Anticrop weapons* and *CBW* (chemical and biological warfare) posed threats to "friendly" troops as well as enemies, as the *Agent Orange* experience showed.

Surface-to-air missiles became more compact so it required only a few soldiers to fire them. *Antimissile missiles* remained problematic, and the *ABM* was probably just a dream. Electronic surveillance of battlefields was increased through military satellites and *AWACS* planes, which could direct theater weapons to their proper targets. For such tasks, "small" nuclear weaponry was devised, increasing reliance on nuclear arms and reinforcing the "bomb logic" which seemed inescapable.

Theoretical Puzzles

Even as science and technology occupied a privileged position in the culture, the boundaries of knowledge were being extended toward puzzling new phenomena which threatened the coherence of *mainstream* scientific models.

Largely unnoticed in the furor over atomic bombs and nuclear energy was the fact that the "atom" had been supposed to be the ultimate particle, the indivisible building block of nature. However, it was not, as research into the atom discovered numerous *high-energy particles*, one of which was named the *strange particle*, which seemed to be smaller than atoms. How were these smaller particles held together? Science could do no better than hypothesize *gluons*, sticky sub-particles to paste together the formerly indivisible atom.

Light of course, continued to be a mystery—early twentieth century physics had been unable to decide whether it was a particle or a wave, and calling it a "wavicle" did not solve the dilemma. Still, the speed of light was supposed to be the maximum speed of all particles in the universe, until it became theoretically possible to hypothesize *tachyons*, particles travelling faster than light.

The inability to characterize light as either a particle or a wave spilled over into discussions of gravity. Was gravity an exchange of *gravitons*, or was it a *gravitational wave*? Both sides were argued.

The universe itself became more puzzling. *Radio galaxies* were discovered which were only "visible" to radio telescopes. *Black holes* were hypothesized to exist, but since light could not escape from them, they were impossible to find on instruments. There were theoretical reasons to predict *time dilation* and even *time reversal* under some conditions. There was still disagreement over whether the universe had started with a *big bang*, or gone along forever in a *steady state*. There was evidence to support both sides.

Scientific theory in our period failed to provide answers to basic questions about the universe it was studying. Worse, it seemed to confuse issues more. Just as the solutions of technology became problematic, so did the underlying theoretical solutions.

Summary

The all-pervasiveness of technology can be seen in the bewildering variety of terms it produced in the period from 1961 to 1986. In a culture which routinely calls upon technology for a quick *fix*, we find it applied to areas as personal as birth control and as impersonal as outer space.

Yet the *fixes* have led to problems of their own. The *IUD*, for example, had to be *recalled* because of the health problems it caused. *The pill* may become dangerous because it allows the transmission of *AIDS*. The sexual behavior implied by birth control technologies has produced a political *backlash*, often taking the form of opposition to technologies of abortion.

A similar mixture of desirable and undesirable results, foreseen and unforeseen effects, can be found with all the major technological "miracles" described by our new words. The atom has produced bigger bangs for a buck, but also life-threatening *fallout* from tests and power plants which does not discriminate between friend and foe. The exploration of space is being pushed by the superpowers, but may result in the erosion of all national power, as satellites can "see" and broadcast with no regard for national boundaries.

Computers will speed up tasks of computation, but may make many jobs obsolete, particularly when allied with the new science of *robotics*.

And the theoretical advances of science have posed central and serious questions about the nature of the universe which have not been answered.

In these words, then, we have a map of a very problematic territory. Technological change has, indeed, changed experience, in ways the language is still struggling to describe. While we do not understand our complex technology, we depend upon it, and call on it to solve the most diverse problems. We are thus caught in the self-perpetuating logic of the "techno-trap," producing new problems as we seek to solve old ones.

CHAPTER FOUR

New Lifestyles Terms

A Shopping Mall of Words

The technologically augmented world-spanning consumer society produced an "awesome" variety of goods during our period. Lifestyles proliferated, producing almost one in four of the new words in the dictionary *12,000 Words*. (See Table 3.)

The biggest stories in Lifestyles were the increases in available types of "Food" (4 percent of the new words), "Clothing and other terms" (3.9 percent), and "Sports and Fitness" (2.8 percent).

Yet the most controversy surrounded three categories which, appropriately enough, tied in our sample with 1.6 percent of the new words: "Sex," "Drugs," and "Music—all types." Formerly taboo sexual and drug subcultures added their terms to the general language, often with some domestication of their rough edges. Thus one could speak of being a sports *freak*, or an ice cream *junkie*, in a humorous vein. Yet such "drugspeak" implied a tendency to addiction, dependency, and a craving for extraordinary states of consciousness which seemed to be the dark underside of the consumer culture's search for the new.

Clearly, this is a culture in the grip of *neophilia*, or love of the new. With the mass media constantly promoting the latest, new improved products; with the economy geared to producing soon-to-be-obsolete fashionable consumer goods, and with the need for distraction from the *politicization* of life (discussed in Chapter 5), it is not surprising that this period produced a culture of *neophiliacs*.

As a result, there was a constant desire, particularly among the baby boomers, to be *trendy, zingy*, have the *in* look, have a little *pizazz*, be *something else, mod*, or *drop-dead chic. Gimmicky* new products were sought out in the effort to be *extraordinaire. Frabjous* styles produced *gee-whiz* looks and *glitzy* fashions were labeled as *fantabulous*.

One result of this preoccupation with showing off the new, was a tendency for people to perform for each other, even in situations which formerly had been private or intimate and personal. In

Table 3. *LIFESTYLES TERMS*

Rank	No. Words	Category	% Words
7	219	Food	4.095
9	209	Generic Lifestyles	3.908
12	154	Sports	2.880
16	86	Drugs—Illicit	1.608
16-tie	86	Music—All Types	1.608
16-tie	86	Sex	1.608
19	76	Automobiles	1.421
21	55	Television	1.028
24	43	Animals	0.804
26	37	Religion, Spirituality, Astrology	0.691
28	32	Art	0.598
28-tie	32	Literature	0.598
29	30	General Media Terms	0.561
31	26	Movies	0.486
32	24	Records, Tapes, CDs	0.448
33	20	Journalism	0.374
34	19	Aircraft	0.355
36	15	Telephones	0.280
37	14	Pop Culture—General	0.261
37-tie	14	Theater	0.261
38	10	Radio	0.187
39	7	Advertising	0.130
TOTAL	1294		24.190

Meyrowitz's (1985) terms, using the imagery of Goffman (1959), what was formerly "backstage" behavior (private, intimate) moved increasingly "frontstage" (public). Or we might say that "frontstage" invaded "backstage" areas of life, with a little help from technology. If you weren't careful to *debug* your bedroom, you might find your "backstage" life very "frontstage" indeed.

Food

This has been the era of *fast food* and *junk food*; prepackaged *convenience foods*, *TV dinners*, and *take-out*. Technology has been applied to such monuments of eating efficiency as the *corn chip* and the *megavitamin*. In such an environment, one hardly eats, one *scarfs* one's food.

If you had the *munchies*, it was easy to *pig out*, and many people found themselves overweight candidates for the *fat farm*, or various weight-control programs like *aerobics* to get rid of the *cellulite*. For others, eating took on the status of a life-threatening disorder, as *anorexics* did not eat at all, and *bulimics* ate only to *barf* it all up in a spasm of guilt.

To deal with this issue of weight, all sorts of *lite* foods were produced in the 1980s; leading to speculation that this was the *lite* decade, where you could eat (or consume) more, but get less out of it.

The *counterculture* substituted *vegeburgers* for hamburgers, and some people willingly gave up meat diets for strictly *vegan* diets (consuming no animal products). Such nonconformity was often considered *out-to-lunch*, but as the period progressed, *mainstream* diets started to contain less meat and potatoes, and *salad bars* began appearing in restaurants and supermarkets.

Natural foods and *health foods* like the soy-based *tofu, tempeh,* and *soy milk* became more visible in *upscale* diets as well as *counterculture* fare. *Granola* and *gorp* became popular with more than *backpackers*.

There was also an influx of international foods, as more Americans enjoyed *stir frying* in their *wok*, or filling *pita bread* with *hummus*. Middle Eastern foods like *tahini, felafel,* and *gyros* were especially popular. But names of foods from many countries, such as *babka, cannoli, coquille St. Jacques, refried beans,* and Amerindian *fry bread* enter the dictionary in this period.

Clothes

The stylistic eclecticism of this period is well captured in the three names for skirt lengths: the *mini,* the *midi,* and the *maxi*. There was no one style which was clearly *in,* and it was acceptable to get outrageously *campy*.

The entrance of women into the work world in increasing numbers led to the popularity of the *pant suit* and easy to manage *pantyhose*. There was a blurring of formerly distinct types of clothes in the *shirtdress* and the *shirt jacket*. The *jumpsuit* was comfortable, while *granny dresses* and *granny glasses* de-emphasized sexuality. *Capri pants, hot pants,* and *hip huggers,* however, emphasized it.

Some *libbers* went *braless* to protest the confining styles of clothes. *Black nationalists* wore *dashikis* to emphasize African roots, and *Mao jackets* or *Nehru jackets* implied *Third World* loyalties.

Fitness and Sports

The country became fitness conscious, as attested to by the popularity of *jogging* and *aerobics. Bikeways* were constructed so bicyclists could ride their *ten-speeds* safely away from traffic. *Body-builders pumped iron* or did *isometric exercises.* Afterwards there was relaxation in the *Jacuzzi* (trademark) or *hot tub.* The *Frisbee* (trademark) became popular in these years.

The only major sports which send large numbers of new terms into the dictionary are football and surfing. Probably the mass media, television for football, and records and movies for surfing, were the main sources for these terms; for neither sport was widely participated in.

Football provided terms like *look-in pass, double reverse, delay, blitzing,* and *keeper.* A roving linebacker was a *monster back.* Kickoff and return teams were the *suicide squad.*

Surfing provided the term *hot dogging* (showing off) which has since become quite general in application. You can *kick out* and *shoot the curl* (surf into the hollow arch under the crest of a wave) if you aren't a *gremmie* (inexperienced surfer). It's OK to be a *beach bunny* (nonsurfing girl), but not a *hodad* (one who pretends to be a surfer).

Other sports contributed some new terms: *slam dunk* from basketball, *designated hitter* from baseball, and *slap shot* from hockey.

On a more general level, a vocabulary of games and game-playing became "executive talk" in this period, as discussed later. Competitive sports became a metaphor for the uncertain managerial landscape of the technological society.

Drugs

A striking feature of the language of post-World War II America is the entrance into the *mainstream* dictionaries of the terminology from subcultures of drug-users and *alternative* sexual preferences.

Until around 1950, according to Maurer and High (1980), the argot of the drug subculture was secret from most Americans. Now, however, we may use such terms as *uptight* and *strung out* with no awareness of their drug subculture origins.

The reasons for the migration of terms from a subculture into the mainstream culture are complex (see Halliday, 1978). If the subculture interacts increasingly with the dominant culture, some terms start to slip through into the dominant vocabulary. Yet there must be an interest in the *mainstream* culture in those words—they must fulfill a role in the life of the culture which none of its presently accredited words can do. This is the "functional" view, described by Aitchison (1981).

The rush of terms from sex and drug subcultures indicates that the *mainstream* culture became more involved with these subcultures and also that in some ways the *mainstream* experience mirrored the subculture experience, requiring words from the subculture to describe it. However, often, the subcultural terms became transformed in meaning as they entered the *mainstream*.

For example, two drug subculture terms about addiction—*junkie*, and *strung out*—have become domesticated to mean something less than addiction in mainstream use. We hear humorous references to *junk food junkies* without reflecting on the less-than humorous origin of the term; and we hear songs about being *strung out* over you as a colorful way of describing an emotional state. Yet the use of these terms implies something about the quality of experience in *mainstream* life—perhaps that we have become needy and require our *fixes* (another drug term) in many different ways.

Other terms from the drug subculture which have become "domesticated" in *mainstream* use are *turn on, trip, blow one's mind, flip out,* and *freak out*. In the original subcultural uses, these referred to taking drugs (*turn on*), having a visionary experience (*trip*), with intense emotional excitement (*mind-blowing*), losing self-control (*flip out*), and behaving irrationally (*freak out*). In the "domesticated" uses, they can refer to becoming pleasurably stimulated (*turn on*), by the pursuit of an absorbing interest or way of life (*trip*) which can sometimes take you by surprise (*blow your mind*) and cause you to become even more enthusiastic (*flip out*) although you try not to lose your composure (*freak out*).

In the above examples, the subculture use of the terms is more emotionally extreme than the *mainstream* uses. And yet the subculture terms have carried something of the quality of drug experiences with them. In many ways the language used to describe drug experiences came to be felt appropriate for describing life in the *mainstream*: a sense of dependency, a need for release from tension, a search for *mind-expanding* insights.

As we know, the Post-World War II period saw an unprecedented amount of drug use in the society. First hitting middle-class suburbia in the 1960s, by the 1970s drugs had spread down to elementary schools. Just how the tremendous volume of illegal materials entered the country was a question never satisfactorily answered. Yet the market would not have been there if there hadn't been a need for the *mind-blowing* experiences drugs could provide.

One could get *mellow* and *laid back* by *toking* on a *joint* of *grass*, maybe *Acapulco Gold*. Drugs could provide a *mind-expanding trip* or a *downer*. You could get "chemical highs" from *glue-sniffing* or serious disorientation from *angel dust*. Cocaine could be *sniffed*, *shot*, or *freebased*. *Acid* produced *psychedelic* experiences which were portrayed in *acid rock* and colorful *way out* art. Users of *hard drugs* like heroin would *shoot* some *stuff* (or *shit*) and *nod* out.

Too much drugs would leave you *spaced out*, *zonked*, *wasted*, *whacked*, or *wrecked*. If you weren't careful you could get *strung out*, and become a *junkie*. These terms came to apply not only to drug-related hangovers, but to alcohol hangovers and depressed states in general. Once again the subcultural experience provided useful terms for *mainstream* experience.

It is interesting to note that during this period, more "new" terms enter the language from drugs than from alcohol; although overall, there are many more terms for being *smashed* (drunk) than being *stoned*. You may get *sloshed* and *86'd* from a bar, and if you get caught *DWI* (driving while intoxicated), you'll get jailed to *dry out* and *detoxify*. But most of the glamor vocabulary describing altered states of consciousness comes from drugs.

Sex

A large number of sexually related words entered the dictionary in our period, providing perhaps the most dramatic example of backstage behavior moving frontstage. Many of these were older terms from the *gay* subcultures or from what used to be called "vulgar slang." So it is not that these terms were invented in our period which makes them significant, but that they became such a part of the written and "respectable" language that they had to be included in dictionaries.

At the risk of offending some readers' sensibilities, I would like to illustrate this movement of backstage terms to frontstage by discussing the "f word," formerly known as "f—," but now dragged into the full light of day as *fuck*. This old Anglo-Saxon word did not appear in the controversial 1961 *Webster's Unabridged*, nor the 7th Edition *Collegiate Dictionary* (1963). After the raucous 1960s, however, the word made its way into the *Collegiate* dictionaries, and even into the conservative *American Heritage Dictionary Second College Edition* (Houghton-Mifflin, 1979). The *Collegiate* dictionaries labeled it as "usually considered obscene," and the *American Heritage Dictionary* as "obscene," just to let us know that even permissive linguists disapproved. But there it was—alone and in glorious combinations.

If you *fucked* with someone, you might copulate with them or you might interfere unfairly or harshly with them—an interesting juxtaposition of meanings. A situation can be *fucked-up* and a person can be a *fuckup*—another term for incompetents which proliferate during our period. If you're exploited you're *fucked over*, and if you want someone to get out you can tell them to *fuck off*.

Other sexual behavior came frontstage as well, especially *gay* culture, where many *closet queens came out*, and organized politically and publicly a *gay liberation* movement. Terms from the *gay* subcultures like *butch, femme, bull dyke, fag hag, nelly, auntie*, and *rough trade* came into general use. People became classified as either *homophobes* or *homophiles*.

Other sexual minorities, such as *S & M* (sadism and masochism) fetishists, and *cross-dressers*, or *TVs* (transvestites), found their place in the dictionary; along with *pansexuals* and *ambisextrous* or *bi* persons, also known as *switch hitters* or *AC/DC*. Different variations on the sex act came out of the linguistic *closet* as well. The *missionary position* was *out*. *Group gropes* and *daisy chains* were supposedly engaged in by *swingers*.

The *singles* life, of *cruising* and going to *dating bars* looking for *bunnies, dishy divorcees*, or *hunks*, could lead to *making out*, or *scoring*, even if only a *one-night stand*. Birth control technologies like the *pill*, the *loop*, or the *morning-after pill* freed people from *hang-ups* about pregnancy, although those practicing the rhythm method of birth control played *Vatican Roulette*. If people did *sleep around*, this led to concerns about *STD's* (sexually transmitted diseases) such as the *herpes virus* and *AIDS*, a *retrovirus* which appeared in the 1970s.

Patterns of living together changed, even in *hetero, straight* culture. When the wife worked, men became *house husbands*. Some people experimented with *open marriages*. Others lived together without being married, causing linguistic embarrassment when no appropriate term existed to describe the relationship. This did not stop former "roommates" from suing one another upon separation, particularly if they were celebrities, and getting widely publicized *palimony* settlements.

The proliferation of *hard-core* and *soft-core adult* movies, bars with *exotic* dancers, and *sexploitation* in the media generally produced a *backlash*. *Women's liberation* attacked pornography as being *masculinist* and *chauvinist*, and called for a *nonsexist* society. A *pro-life* movement against legalized abortion gained political momentum in the 1970s and 1980s, opposed by *pro-choice* activists who accused them of being *anti-sex*. *Natalists* were opposed to all interruption of conception and birth.

With these debates, and with the growing concern about *AIDS* in the 1980s, choices and behaviors which had been private were dragged irrevocably into the bright light of frontstage.

Automobiles

Over the course of the twentieth century, Americans' love of automobiles has been perhaps the major distinguishing element in their social history. The dream of a car for everyone, considered wildly impractical in 1900, hovered near realization in the post-World War II years. By this time, an automobile had become a necessity for daily living for much of the population, and was almost taken for granted, until energy *crunches* reminded people how vulnerable this "techno-trap" could make them.

As a result, in the 1970s and 1980s, people dropped their old *gas guzzlers*, and bought *downsize, economy* cars. The big convertible gave way to the little *fastback*. The *commute* was more often done in *carpools*. Some cities even blocked off areas to cars, to *pedestrianize* them. Big, flashy cars became suspect as *pimpmobiles*.

But *automania* continued for some. *Vanners* drove customized vans, others lived in their *motor homes*. Campers packed up their *tent trailers* and explored the back roads, *shunpiking* their way around the countryside, making *pit stops* for the kids. People took pride in their *vanity plates*.

The language also gained some terms expressing an increased awareness of the dangers of driving, which claimed approximately 50,000 lives annually during our period (United States Department of Commerce, 1975, 1984). You might get a *ding* in a *fender-bender*, or be *crunched* in a *rear-ender*. The worst accidents were *fatals*, where the car also got *totaled*. The other great hazard was the *Denver Boot*, which might appear on your car if you let too many parking tickets go.

Still, through this period, Americans kept telling each other to *keep on truckin'*—they actually had few other options.

Television

The other great "miracle technology" of the post-World War II era is television. Winston (1986) in keeping with his "law" of the suppression of radical potential of new technologies by existing institutions, notes that this occurred with television. The first TV broadcasts occurred in the 1920s, and Germany and Britain had working TV stations in the 1930s. Yet it was not until the "players" in the radio and electronics industries had worked out accommodations among themselves that television appeared on any scale in this country.

TV spread rapidly in the late 1940s and the 1950s, becoming known as the *boob tube*, or *tube*, and (in *9,000 Words*) as the *idiot box*, or *box*. The implications of these terms are interesting. First, a *boob* in one definition is a stupid person, an idiot—implying that people of low intelligence watch TV. This is an interesting commentary since almost everyone did watch TV. But *boob* in another definition and *box* are both vulgar terms for portions of the female anatomy. This implies that in the language TV is covertly constructed as feminine. (In a perhaps unrelated development, *TV* is a subcultural term for transvestite, a man in woman's clothes. The author has unable to discover whether the subcultural use of *TV* predates television.)

The terminology of *videoland* (the television industry or TV as a medium) has proliferated with the complexity of the technology. Only a few of its specialized terms have entered the dictionary in our period. The *line-up* of *prime time* shows is news each season, along with the strategies for *counterprogramming* between the networks on *sweeps weeks*, seeking to maximize *viewership*.

On-camera, the old *talking head* approach has been jazzed up with *isolated cameras, freeze frames,* and other *camerawork* techniques. *Off camera, pre-* and *post-production* work with *videotape* on advanced *decks,* allows *edits, jump cuts, flashbacks, voice-overs,* and *bleeps* to be inserted unobtrusively.

The increased sophistication of *videotape* technology has made the industry reluctant to do material *live,* in *real time.* Instead, *video vérité* effects are created in *postproduction.*

The economics of the medium are driven by *admass* (mass advertising), creating *hot* products for the *upscale demographics.* Searching for the right *media mix* to reach specialized *markets,* some advertisers supported *narrowcasting,* on *CATV* (cable television) and *pay cable,* others relied on old shows in *syndication* or on *superstations.* Extensive research paired shows to ads, with different approaches called for on *kid vid, sitcoms, miniseries, TV magazines, talk shows, shoot-em-ups,* and *family movies.*

The result has been a tremendous explosion of *pop culture,* and an expansion of *midcult* (middlebrow culture). This area has been increasingly accepted as worthy of serious study, although the suspicion remained that a *situation comedy* was to real comedy as a *TV Dinner* was to a real dinner.

Meanwhile, with the help of *communication satellites, cable TV, closed-circuit TV,* and *pay TV,* television was breaking its old boundaries. New material, some of it *X-rated,* could be seen on *home screen* TV. You could get information from a computer *database* on TV with *videotex.* You could play your own *videotapes* on the *VCR* (video cassette recorder), and *zap* commercials using your remote control.

Combined with telephone lines, especially the new *optical fibers, videoconferences* became possible, as well as other connections with computers into *interactive cable* systems.

While *McLuhanesque* terminology labeled television as a *cool* medium, its frenetic pacing and penchant for violent programming caused many to suspect that it heated up the society, rather than cooling it down.

Spirituality

This period also saw a growth of *alternative* spirituality, as cults like the *Hare Krishnas* and *Moonies* grew in numbers, and *Jesus Freaks* appeared preaching on street corners. The *Rastafarians* spread their ideas from Jamaica through their *reggae* music and advocation of marijuana use as a sacrament. Ashrams and *Zendos* opened for spiritual life and meditation. *Born-again* and *charismatic* Christians grew in numbers also.

The methods of all cults came into question after the mass murder and suicide in Jonestown in the 1970s. Some parents had their children kidnapped from the cults so they could be *deprogrammed*.

More quietly, people began practicing relaxation techniques like *Transcendental Meditation, holistic* health practices like *acupressure* and *rolfing*, oriental exercise systems, like yoga and *tai chi*, and martial arts like karate and *tae kwan do*. Businesses scheduled *T-groups* (training groups) for their staff to take *sensitivity training*. People joined *encounter groups* of different psychological schools, and the women's movement started *consciousness-raising* groups.

Witches met in *esbats* and practiced *astral projection*. Students of yoga tried to elevate their *kundalini energy* and activate their body *chakras*. People of all sorts discussed their astrological signs, all of which enter the dictionary during this period.

Art, Literature and Theater

The United States became the world center for painting in the 1950s with the emergence of *action painting* by Pollock, Tobey, and others. Painting for the sake of action seemed appropriate in the frantic world of post-World War II America. Abstraction was further developed in *hard-edge painting,* and *minimal,* or *ABC art* which used basic geometric forms in unadorned styles. *Op art* rested on optical illusions, and *conceptual art* played on figure-ground reversals.

Pop art, as developed by Warhol and others, glorified the technological environment of consumer culture by monumentalizing some of its more mundane products. *Photo-realism* took the technological environment into account in another way—it attempted to make paintings into replicas of photographs.

A response to the *throwaway* culture was found in *junk art,* using *found objects*. The style of focusing in on small, concrete areas of reality came to be called *verismo*.

This focus on small units of reality also appeared in the theater, where it led to *absurdist* plays, *black comedy* with *gallows humor, Pinteresque neo-Dada* theater which expressed no hope of ever making sense out of the social environment.

Meanwhile the confines of Broadway were too small for the times, and *off-Broadway* and *off-off-Broadway* theater appeared; along with *street theater* and *guerrilla theater* with a decidedly political tinge. This was also the period of *method acting*, where actors blurred the distinctions between their play characters and their "real" characters—not unlike what was occurring in the society at large.

In literature, despite the advent of television, Americans were still willing to give their authors a *read*, and some authors' names made it into the language as symbolic of certain ideas or styles.

Orwellian refers to the author's novel *1984*, both terms conjuring up images of totalitarianism and *Newspeak*. *Kafkaesque* and *Pinteresque* refer to *absurdism* highlighted by these authors. *Catch-22* brings *black comedy* to bureaucracy.

Faulknerian doubtless refers to long, convoluted, *arabesque* sentences, while *Hemingwayesque* refers to a more terse, telegraphic style, or perhaps a *macho* image. *Nabokovian* refers to colorful marginal people or sexually tempting young girls. *Wildean* wit and sophistication are memorialized in the term; while *Brechtian* sternness and realism are at the opposite pole.

McLuhanesque refers to collages of obscure but witty observations about media and culture. *Skinnerian* implies a philosophy of environmental conditioning. *Galbraithian* has become a *code word* for economic liberalism, as *Friedmanite* is for economic conservatism.

Also included as authors under the *auteur* theory of filmmaking would be Alfred Hitchcock and the *Hitchcockian* mystery and suspense genre he exemplified; and Walt Disney and the *Disneyesque* fantasies he animated.

Film

Film became positively highbrow during the period studied, with *cinema vérité* and *film noir* techniques influencing still photography and television, *New Wave Cinema* inspiring *auter theory* and spurring research into the *filmography* of directors. *Cinemaphiles* were admitted into the ranks of the *culturati* as journals of film criticism proliferated.

There were still, of course, *mass cult* products like the *spaghetti westerns*, *blaxploitation* films, various *shoot-em-ups*, and *family movies*. These often relied on *bankable superstars* or their cheaper *look-alikes*. *Underground movies* continued to be made as well, although they did not make it into the flashy new *cinematheques*.

Most controversial were the *sexploitation* films, both *soft-core* and *hard-core porn*. These *skin flicks* or *nudies* aroused opposition from communities containing *X-rated* theaters; until, in the 1980s, the *sexploitation* market discovered the *VCR*.

Journalism

The new terminology of journalism, both print and electronic, shows the influence of media issues between 1961 and 1986. This is a time when judges issue *gag orders* to keep media out, and *sunshine laws* are passed to let media in. Media make the *whistleblower* possible, and *shield laws* are passed to protect them and reporters, as they attempt to expose *cover-ups*.

However, TV news shows have focused more on *mediagenic anchorpersons*, and less on *in-depth* coverage or *profiles*. *Media events*, *pseudo-events*, and *non-events* have taken up more and more *air time*, leading critics like Postman (1985) to charge that television has trivialized political discourse in this country.

Print news also became more visual with the *photo essay*, more sensationalistic with *gee-whiz* journalism, and downright *zonked* with *gonzo* journalism (a style of journalism that is a mix of fact and fiction and is held to be produced under the influence of drugs).

Fact and fiction get blurred in the *New Journalism* in print, as well as in *docudramas* on television. Straight *advocacy journalism* has tended to be relegated to the *underground press*, while the *establishment* press is accused of practicing *checkbook journalism* (paying for interviews and information), and *Afghanistanism* (covering distant problems while ignoring controversial local issues).

In such an environment, *disinformation* flourishes, and we see a tendency to follow the latest *buzz words* rather than take time for *in-depth backgrounders*.

Radio and Rock Music

In the 1950s radio, which had been the nation's major mass medium, lost most of its listeners to TV. It survived by a sort of *narrowcasting*, specializing in rock 'n' roll for the rebellious young, news and music for *drive-time* audiences, and an alliance with the alarm clock in the *clock radio*. The *transistor radio* became truly portable.

This formula succeeded so well that by the 1970s and 1980s, the old lower-class rock songs became *golden oldies,* and the exuberance of American music was perhaps the high point of cultural creativity in this period. *Chartbusters* were churned out by *supergroups* regularly. The *Top 40* became a medley of *soft rock, hard rock, punk rock, progressive rock, new wave rock, heavy metal, disco,* and *folk-rock.* There were separate charts for *soul music,* and *country (C & W)* or *rockabilly;* although these performers made it onto the *Top 40* as well. More esoteric *electronic music,* using *Moogs* (trademark) and other *synthesizers,* became popular as more groups turned to them for special effects.

Meanwhile the old *bluesmen* and *folkies* expanded their audiences, even if they were nowhere near *superstar* status. *Cross-over* styles like *jazz-rock* and *folk-rock* became popular, and regional styles like *zydeco* were heard nationally. Foreign influences from *bossa nova* and *salsa* music increased. The bland *Muzak* (trademark) appeared in stores and elevators everywhere.

Controversy swirled around some songs, especially *psychedelic* rock, which was thought to glamorize drug experiences; and popular music was certainly an important channel conveying words from drug subcultures to the society at large.

Meanwhile, recording studios and their technology became important gates to upward mobility, as they provided their facilities to make *demos* to impress *A & R* people (Artist and Repertory staff from record companies). A good *master tape, mixed* on a *high-tech deck,* using *overdubs* and *reverbs,* could make all the difference to a young *rocker.* Without the technology, even a *tight* performance of *finger-popping* music wouldn't appeal to the *bubble gum groupies.*

Summary

The affluent society has clearly been grinding out a bewildering variety of consumer goods, from food and clothes to automobiles and drugs between 1961 and 1986. A greater variety of lifestyles became available, and formerly taboo *gay* and drug subcultures emerged into *mainstream* awareness.

Yet this variety of lifestyles did not produce social harmony. Quite the opposite, there emerged social tension and the *politicization* of many areas of life. And the new world economy proved to be puzzling and unpredictable. We will turn to these areas in the next chapters.

CHAPTER FIVE

New Words from the Economy and Society

Complexity and Contentiousness

New words describing social and economic conditions make up 11 percent of the total sample of new words. (See Table 4). Economic terms (4.75 percent) tell a story of a puzzling and complex economy which continually defies the theories put forward to explain it. Executives, faced with the necessity of making choices, developed a richly metaphorical vocabulary of game-playing and *hardball* maneuvers to conceptualize the new situation. However, as we look at this vocabulary in the section on "Executalk," it is worth wondering if such a vocabulary of *hard-eyed* toughness could ever produce socially responsible behavior.

The growing contentiousness of society appears in the social terms (2 percent) and political terms (1.8 percent). *Politicization* in *technopolis* was covered in Chapter 1. Here we will look at the struggles between the *plastic* culture of consumerism and the newly emerging *environmentalist* critiques.

Table 4. *SOCIAL-ECONOMIC TERMS*

Overall Rank	No. Words	Category	% Words
5	254	Economy	4.750
13	108	Society	2.019
15	97	Politics—All Types	1.814
16	86	Schools	1.608
25	38	Ethnic & Minority Terms	0.710
30	28	General Soc-Ec Terms	0.523
TOTAL	611		11.424

The Complex Economy

Boosted by World War II, the United States economy pulled itself out of the Great Depression and produced an expanding consumer paradise through the 1950s and 1960s. For a few giddy years, it seemed that all citizens might be brought into the folds of prosperity. But in the late 1960s and 1970s, the quagmire in Vietnam, shrinking corporate profit margins, Arab oil embargoes, and *double-digit* inflation in conjunction with *sub-employment* producing *slumpflation*, all combined to puncture this *postmodern American Dream*. In the belt-tightening 1980s, earlier economic assumptions of affluence came to have an *Alice-in-Wonderland* appearance.

In this period, the outlines of a new world economy became visible. Corporations became *multinationals*. The world was divided up in *neocolonial* fashion into:

—the *First World* (Western, industrialized, non-Communist nations);
—the *Second World* (Communist bloc nations);
—the *Third World* (*developing* nations);
—the *Fourth World* (underdeveloped nations with nothing to export).

These categories proved far too simplistic, as, for example, Russia and China split in the *Second World*, and as OPEC made some *Third World* countries fabulously wealthy. The oil crises of the 1970s tightened the "techno-trap," and sparked another division of the world, into the oil-producing and the *non-oil nations. Petrodollars* and *petropolitics* redefined domestic and world power in ways only becoming visible gradually to Americans used to thinking of themselves as a superpower.

The trend toward *multinationalism*, assisted by global communications technology, spurred talk of the *deindustrialization* of America, as the old *smokestack* industries found their production tasks being shifted overseas to the factories of friendly *client states*. What was good for General Motors was not necessarily any longer good for the United States. Increasingly, defense and electronic industries relied on imported goods.

At home, a century-long trend toward economic concentration continued, unabated by periodic efforts at anti-trust. *Conglomerates* formed and re-formed with dizzying speed in the atmosphere of *deregulation* in the 1980s. Some of the *multi-industry* deals were frankly *anti-competitive*, others produced *dinosaurs* which needed to be *downsized*. A new breed of *power broker* came into prominence, sometimes playing *dirty pool* in their *adversarial* tactics to *score* unfriendly takeovers. These *conglomerators* often offered *excessed* executives *golden parachutes* to soften the blow of being suddenly *dehired*.

In this shifting environment, *old money* apparently managed to retain the central positions in the *establishment*, but there was a growing *new guard* which commanded a *piece of the action*. In the new *technostructure*, *credentialism* demanded that one *pay one's dues* by getting advanced degrees. *Upward mobility* depended on one's *track record*, so there was a good deal of *job-hopping*. This posed a problem of a *brain drain*, for many companies as well as some countries. To deal with disorganization sometimes bordering on being *non-systems*, companies formed *adhocracies* and did less of their work *in-house*.

Corporations put large amounts of money into *R & D* (research and development), looking for *spinoffs* and *follow-on products* from their research. Operations were *computerized* to cut down *turnaround time*. *Systems analysts strategized game plans* so the company would not be *nickel and dimed* to death by its new *capital-intensive* technologies.

Many decisions involved difficult *trade-offs*, with *toss-up* choices, *dicey* outcomes, and unpredictable *ripple effects*. There was the danger of *overresponding* and *overshooting* the mark, or not doing enough and getting forced *up against the wall* in the *crunch*, and going back to *square one*, or perhaps getting a government *bailout*.

Through it all, everyone was looking out for *numero uno*. It was an age of *situation ethics*. In the presence of the *megamachine*, many otherwise responsible people were tempted to do jobs *quick and dirty*, *skim* something off the top, *launder* the money, and hide any *smoking guns* in a *cover-up*. Honest and dishonest, it became wise to keep a *low profile* and not *make waves*. No wonder many felt *cognitive dissonance* or *future shock*.

Puzzles

The new large, complex economy proved puzzling in many respects. Measures which once had seemed sound, now became *counterproductive.* Large systems sometimes behaved in ways that were *counterintuitive.* A small literary industry emerged to describe such situations, adding a crop of new books and new words to the language.

There was *Murphy's Law,* which stated that if anything can go wrong, it will. When dealing with increasingly complex systems, this phenomenon became more inevitable.

Then there was *Parkinson's Law,* which noted that the amount of office work expands so as to fill the time available for its completion. This gave some insight into the frustrating inability to cut back on bureaucracy met by both government and industry in this period.

The *Peter Principle* cut a little deeper: it claimed that in a bureaucracy a person was promoted to his/her level of incompetence. If you did your job well, you got promoted, taking you out of that job and putting you in another job. If you did that well, you got promoted out of that one, and so on, until you reached a job in which you were incompetent. There you would stay.

Then there was *Catch-22,* a novel about the military which abounded with *absurdist* consequences of bureaucratic organization. In general usage, the term has come to mean:

—a problematic situation for which the only solution is denied by an inherent circumstance or by a rule;
—an illogical, unreasonable, or senseless situation;
—a measure or policy whose effect is the opposite of that intended;
—a situation presenting two equally undesirable alternatives;
—a hidden difficulty: catch.

Faced with all these, it is understandable if some people and organizations experienced *future shock,* and were unable to cope with the rapid social and technological changes.

Executalk

Behind all these insights, we can sense a deep need for control in the new complex economy. In the *counterintuitive* environment, if you don't want to go *belly-up,* you'd better have control.

Therefore, in this period there emerged a vocabulary for coping with such indeterminate and uncertain situations. The author calls this vocabulary Executalk. Many of its terms clustered around the metaphor of a "game." Perhaps this came from game theory, developed mathematically in the 1950s to describe business and military situations. Or perhaps it came from the popularity of sports on television, particularly with *upscale honchos* from the business world.

However, the game metaphor is instructive, for it implies an emphasis on performance as the essential value. Who you are is less important than how you have performed in your last *ball game*. What you know doesn't matter unless you can bring it into play.

And what is the *name of the game* (essential quality of the situation, fundamental goal)? Let's call this one *hardball* (forceful or uncompromising methods used).

If you want a *piece of the action*, you'll need a *game plan*. Get a *systems analyst* to *computerize* a *scenario*. Is it a *can of worms*, or a *piece of cake*? *Strategize* so you won't *overrespond*. *Prioritize cost-effective modules* in each *time frame*. Bring in staff with a good *track record*.

Before you can get any new system to *fly*, you'll have to surmount the *learning curve*, and expect some *glitches* and *hassles*. You may have to *goose* the project with extra staff so it doesn't turn into a *black hole*. If you *screw up*, you'll wind up with a *clunker* that could send you all *down the tubes*. But if you want to draw *first blood*, and *preempt* the competition, you'll need to get everything *ASAP*.

Sooner or later, the *moment of truth* will arrive. You'll hit the *point of no return*. You'll have to *bite the bullet, grasp the nettle*, make a *go-no-go* decision and *let the chips fall where they may*.

When it comes down to the *crunch*, you're either in *left field* or *on the money*. You hope to get *home free*, that no *wild card* will get played, that nothing will *hit the fan*, blow the whole *ball game* and send you back to *square one*. With this much money invested, you can't give in to *naderism* and issue a *recall*. That would turn into a *holocaust*—the *ripple effects* would put you and your staff on the next *hit list*. This late in the game you get by with *band-aids* (temporary or expedient measures), and maybe *phase down* the more *dicey* aspects of the project. Even if its a *toss-up*, you've got to *hang tough*. *Play it by ear* and *fine tune* what you can, but refuse to *phase out*, so you won't *take a bath*.

If you don't play *hardball*, it will be *open season* on you, and the whole *ball of wax* will come *unglued*. You'll be *dehired, excessed*, and become an *un-person* in short order. That's why, in order to *score* big, and remain a *honcho*, you've got to be a *hardliner*, play by *situation ethics*, and protect your *deniability*. Forget about everything but the *bottom line*.

This dense mini-narrative, constructed from the words of *hardball* players themselves, highlights the key points in the game, and the terms imply what strategies will be used. We do gain some access to the conceptual world of the *hardball* executive: a world of unprincipled competition, full of threatening landmarks and unforeseen pitfalls. An unforgiving world, it requires your best performance at all times. Naturally you will try to anticipate *glitches*, but you will always miss some, as the complex world of business and technology is in many respects unpredictable.

In this bleak *scenario*, survival becomes more important than honesty. Expedient *band-aids* become more attractive than necessary basic reforms. Clearly, in such a reality, using this vocabulary, social responsibility becomes very difficult.

The puzzling nature of the techno-economic reality is further reinforced when we examine the new terms from economic theory in the next section.

Economic Theory

In the 1961 to 1986 period, economists become key advisors to presidents and *power brokers*, and sometimes form their own *adhocracy* within the *technostructure*. They become avid searchers for *indicators* which might bolster their predictions: *leading indicators*, *coincident indicators*, or *lagging indicators* are all sought.

We find economic theorists concerned with inflation, which reached *double-digit* proportions in the 1970s. Theorists were unable to agree on whether inflation was *cost-push* or *demand-pull*. If it is *cost-push*, then it can be fought by keeping costs down, perhaps even by freezing prices. This implies government control over business, and a set of policies termed *Galbraithian* after the economist John Kenneth Galbraith. If, however, inflation is *demand-pull*, then it can only be fought by limiting demand. This can be accomplished by freezing wages, or controlling the money supply, which would increase unemployment, as advocated by *Friedmanite* economists, following the theories of Milton Friedman.

The *new economics* taught the *Phillips Curve*, which stated that inflation and unemployment were inversely related. If high employment produced inflation, the only way to reduce inflation was to increase unemployment. This politically unappealing formula caught decisionmakers in a *double bind,* or *catch-22.* Yet in the 1970s, a period of high inflation was not ended by increasing unemployment, producing the terms *stagflation,* or *slumpflation,* and making the *Phillips Curve* obsolete. Keeping prices high was justified by the notion that corporate profits would *trickle down* to the rest of the population. However, the loss of price elasticity in the *anti-competitive* environment of oligopoly *conglomerates* was a serious matter calling perhaps for an even newer economics to explain it.

Plastic Culture versus Environmentalism

The American experiment in affluence produced a *plastic, disposable, throwaway* culture. *Convenience stores* and *convenience foods* emphasized fulfilling your gratifications quickly. *Shopping malls* brought main street under one roof. The *mall,* the major public architecture of our period, was a *postmodern Xanadu,* available to all with *discretionary income* to spend.

Thus did the new technologically based consumer culture undermine the older values of thrift, hard work, and delayed gratification. These values were relegated to the poor, preached to the *minorities,* and daily violated on the mass media. Instead, presidents declared it a citizen's duty to consume, and the countless advertisements which bombarded each person's consciousness daily reinforced the message.

The old value of the *work ethic*—thrift and delayed gratification— appeared *straight-arrow, dullsville, vanilla.* Instead the culture promoted *neophilia* (love of the new). It became important to be *in, trendy, camp,* and *something else.*

These new values were especially directed toward the *baby boom* generation, who caused a *youthquake* in many sectors of American society—schools, leisure, media, etc. Being *in* came increasingly to mean having brand-name goods, down to items as formerly insignificant as ball point pens, sneakers, blue jeans, and tee shirts. These items did not *make it* without the right logo.

Yet the costs of this consumption lifestyle produced a certain unease in people, accelerated by the energy crises of the 1970s, *acid rain* problems, and a growing awareness of the limited nature of the earth's resources. *Energy budgets* started being discussed, and the *energetics* of the *ecosphere* came under serious study.

Over time, this unease crystallized into various forms of critique of the consumer society, which we might label as broadly *environmentalist*. The terms *ecocide* (destruction of large areas of natural environment) and *ecocatastrophe* (usually human intervention causing massive dislocations in the balance of nature) started to be applied to situations where an earlier generation would have seen only "progress." The increasing *desertification* of formerly arable land was a phenomenon all around the world. Concern grew for *endangered* species, and those who took an uncaring stance about animal suffering were accused of *speciesism*.

The effects of pollutants on the *food pyramid* came to public attention, as traces of *high-tech* pesticides like *dioxin* were found in human populations. The overall effects of technology were predicted to produce a *greenhouse effect*, a heating of the atmosphere especially from *heat islands*, which would have catastrophic *ripple effects*.

The rising *environmentalist* awareness came into conflict with the industrial proponents of the *plastic, disposable* culture more frequently in the 1970s and 1980s. Industry often resisted even relatively mild proposals to install *smogless* technology, or *recycle* waste products. However, the most visible disputes of these years were those over power generation. The industrial forces favored *nukes* and other large-scale electricity generating methods. Environmentalists called for a variety of decentralized sources, such as *solar, wind turbines, cogeneration* (using heat generated as a byproduct in other processes), and even *biogas* to substitute for electricity in some cases.

The *anti-nuclear* forces pointed to the massive *bioenvironmental* consequences of a nuclear power plant accident. The *pro-nuclear* forces threatened the loss of electricity if *nukes* were not built, thus undermining the prosperity of the entire consumer society. *Anti-nuclear* opinions were held to be *anti-science*, and *luddite*.

This tension resulted in a widespread feeling of being both dependent upon technology for an affluent lifestyle, and at the same time threatened by technology. This ambivalent situation has been called the "techno-trap" in Chapter 3.

Being caught in the "techno-trap" seemed to generate an unease which pervaded the *plastic, disposable* culture, and contributed to the general *politicization* of life. Even the smallest act in your kitchen, say, turning on an electric toaster, had a political or ideological tinge. Far from being an age of the end of ideology, it became a time of the domestication and saturation of ideologies.

Schools

As a reaction to the impersonality of the bureaucratic institutions of the *mainstream* culture, advocates of *deinstitutionalization* appeared in areas as diverse as mental health and education, where they called for *deschooling*. While universities grew into *multiversities*, there were efforts to make higher education more personal with *cluster colleges*. There were also efforts to make higher education more accessible, through *open admissions, continuing education* for adults, and *free universities* for *alternative* curricula.

On the elementary school level, *alternative schools* functioned with *open classrooms*, in an effort to replace subject-centered learning with person-centered activities.

However, as the 1980s progressed, there was widespread concern that not only American students but the schools themselves were *underachievers*.

Summary

These words tell a story of a culture becoming much more complex than it had ever been before—courtesy of technology and growing involvement in a world economy. The theme of complexity in American life has not been adequately explored in the literature, although Warsh (1984) discusses it in economics with great insight. He points out that a dollar spent on health care in the 1980s could buy a great deal more variety of services than could one in the 1950s. So have health care costs risen disproportionately? Or do the rising costs accurately reflect the rising complexity of services available? In a period of inflation, such judgments need to be made, yet economic theory is not presently equipped to make them.

Here once again we see technological change undermining the "fit" between language and experience. New words are necessary to map new areas of experience. Yet this change leads to confusion and unpredictability. Decisionmakers are caught in this *crunch*. As a result, they have evolved a vocabulary of game-playing and chance-taking to conceptualize and justify their actions. They have become less concerned with social responsibility and more focused on the *bottom line.*

Meanwhile, the affluent society has been grinding out a bewildering variety of consumer goods, from food and clothes to automobiles and drugs. A greater variety of lifestyles became available, and formerly taboo *gay* and drug subcultures emerged into *mainstream* awareness. Ethnic *minorities* and women also discovered a growing sense of political and economic power.

Yet this variety of lifestyles produced social tension, and the *politicization* of such areas of life as birth control, *throwaway* containers, clothing styles, and religion. The *New Left* of the 1960s, strongly critical of the *plastic* culture, spawned a *New Right* of the 1970s and 1980s, which tried to preserve the old style morality in the new environment.

These tensions produced many derogatory terms for people, which will be discussed in the next chapter.

CHAPTER SIX

Type of People and Actions

Terms of Denunciation

The two categories of "Types of People" and "Types of Action" make up 7 percent of the sample. (See Table 5.)

We have already noted the *politicization* of life which is reflected in and constructed by the language of our period. Not surprisingly, we also find a rich set of new words for denouncing people, and few new words of praise. According to H. L. Mencken (1967), Americans have always been prolific coiners of derogatory phrases, particularly about foreigners and immigrants. But in this recent period of *high tech*, the richest vein of scorn seems to apply to *turkeys* who are incompetent or stupid. There also appear mutually denunciatory vocabularies of *straights* and *freaks*, terms for powerful *honchos*, and for the wealthy *B.P.'s*. Each of these is dealt with in turn.

Table 5. *PEOPLE AND ACTIONS*

Overall Rank	No. of Words	Category	% Words
8	210	Types of People	3.927
11	168	Types of Action	3.141
TOTAL	378		7.068

Incompetent or Stupid Turkeys

The heaviest scorn of the new vocabulary is reserved for those seen to be incompetent or stupid, in other words, those without the requisite skills to perform adequately in a *high-tech* world. The terms minutely code the differences between *turkeys* (stupid, foolish, or inept) and *crazies*, as well as providing a vocabulary of wasting time and error.

If you are a *klutz*, you will take the most *Mickey Mouse* situation and prove what a *screw-up* you are. You probably *futz* around and do things *bass-ackward*. Even the most *rinky-dink* project can be turned into a *clunker* by a *goof-off*.

A *turkey* is usually *out to lunch*, a *schlepper* who *diddles* around but is not too seriously incompetent. A *dipshit* is more serious, an *asshole* who can *fuck up* in dangerous ways.

A *schmuck* is often dishonest, a *scumbag* or a *dork* are vicious, and a *loser* produces *glitches* in everything they touch.

Stupid, naive people are *airheads*, relatively harmless, as are *flakes*. It is a little more threatening to be a *ding-a-ling*, a *dingbat*, a *kook*, or a *wacko*. These are varieties of *crazies* who might get dangerous if they *freak out*. These *sickies* can *do a number on* almost anyone.

You can be intelligent but still be a *nerd* (or *nurd*) (an unpleasant, unattractive, or insignificant person). You might also be a *wimp* (a weak, ineffectual person) or a *nebbish*. More serious is to be a *shithead*, or a *horse's ass*. Maliciousness will earn you the titles of *cocksucker, pisser, fink, rat fink,* or *motherfucker*.

This batch of terms of denunciation indicates that the culture places great store by competence and intelligence, and gets angry at those who do not display those qualities. It is interesting to note that many of the terms use sexual connotations to denounce others. A number of other terms are of Yiddish origin, certainly older than the 1960s, but coming into wider use in the general culture during the 1961–1986 period.

Straights and Freaks

The *politicization* of society by the *counterculture* and the various *neoconservative* responses can be seen in the mutual denunciations between *straights* and *freaks*.

In the 1950s, this division started to appear, as the "beats" and the "squares" started to be spoken of. But it was not until the 1960s that the culture, aided by media representations, started generating these vocabularies.

The term *freak* is interesting, for it carries negative connotations, yet was used by *freaks* themselves as well as *straights* (Landy, 1971). It can mean (as a noun):

—one who uses illicit drugs;
—a hippie, an individualistic rebel; or
—an ardent enthusiast.

We see here a connection between drugs and *hippies,* but also the extension of the term beyond these groups to anyone who gets enthusiastic about something (a sports *freak*). This extension of the term implies that there was something about the experience of being a *freak* which appealed to *mainstream* people, even if they weren't ready to become *hippies.*

Many *freaks,* however, did take drugs, and were called *dopers, heads, potheads, acidheads, pillheads, speed freaks, junkies,* or generically, *druggies.*

Some *flower people* joined cults, and became *Jesus Freaks, Moonies,* or *Hare Krishnas.* Some were *peaceniks,* others became *veggies,* others were *groupies* for *rockers.* Many started as *angry young men* and became *dropouts.*

The *druggies* had their nemesis in the *narcs.* The *bikers* had their nemesis in the *pigs.* The *doves* had their nemesis in the *hawks.*

The *counterculture* developed an ironic vocabulary to describe the *straight* world of *Middle America* from which most of them had come. The *down-home* world of *mom and pop* stores was *dullsville,* full of *lames.* That world expected you to be an *overachiever, tight-assed* with your money, and a *neatnik* with your things. It was best suited for *workaholics* who wanted to be *lifers* in their jobs.

Meanwhile the repressive culture of *Middle America* came to be labeled as *Amerika,* and was seen to produce sexual *hang-ups,* leading men to be *leches* and *dirty old men. Adult* in the period comes to refer to sexually oriented materials.

Meanwhile, the *straights put down* the *weirdos* in the *counterculture. Hippies* were seen as *dingbats, wackos* who couldn't hold down a job or support themselves. There was nothing wrong with being a *nine-to fiver,* and the *druggies* who were *non-starters* were just seen as *losers.*

But the *counterculture* was not the only source of new words describing people in *straight* life. The *straights* produced terms to describe themselves, not all of them complimentary. For example, they noted the increase of *senior citizens,* or *golden agers,* some of whom became *shopping bag ladies.*

As more women joined the workforce, there appeared the *house husband,* and the *latchkey child.* Some women stopped being so concerned to find *Mr. Right,* and settled in to being *bachelorettes.* Some became *libbers,* who signed their name *Ms.,* and fought male *chauvinism.*

Pre-teens dreamed of growing up and becoming *teeny-boppers* and listening to *bubble gum* music. Or perhaps they would become *jocks*, with a sports image, or be *backpackers*, with the wholesome image of an *ecofreak*. You didn't have to be a *black belt* to know you wanted to stay in shape and not be a *fat*. You look great with a tan, so many *snowbirds* became *sunseekers*.

The *straight* world had its answer to the cults with its *born-agains*. It produced its own ardent enthusiasts in *survivalists*. It produced *middle-of-the-roaders* and extremists, like *hard hats* and *Birchers*.

In the working world, it recognized *temps* and *nine to fivers*, and created lowly *gofers*, the new *niggers*.

At the very bottom of the heap, we find *unpersons* (an individual who usually for political or ideological reasons is removed completely from recognition, consideration, or memory) or *nonpersons* (a person regarded as nonexistent). These terms are even below the *antiheroes* and *antiheroines* (protagonists notably lacking in heroic qualities) in the arts of the times.

Powerful Honchos

In the movies, a *heavy* used to be a bad guy, but in post-World War II usage the term came to imply a powerful person, retaining some of its earlier connotations as well. In this period, there appears a vocabulary of powerful people and their ways of coercion, which conveys a mixture of respect and fear.

The *head honcho, numero uno, el supremo,* had a number of ways to *stick it to* you so you'd know who's boss. He/she might *lean on* you, or *put the screws on*. If you *hang tough*, they might take a *hard line* and *kick ass*. Then you might find yourself *deselected*, or *dehired*.

Every organization seems to have its own *mafia*, with its *capo* and *hit man*. You have to stay on the good side of these *power brokers*, because they can *fuck you over*. They are expert *hardball* players, and if you get on their *hit list*, you'll get *messed over*.

Rarely is an *influential* accused of being on an *ego-trip*, or being too *ballsy*. Such criticisms are usually reserved for the *little man* imitating them. Black culture, however, has contributed the words *Mr. Charlie, the man,* and *honky* to criticize such white people in power.

Beautiful People

The other group of people who have achieved some respect, this time mingled with envy, are the so-called *beautiful people* (BP), really referring to wealthy people. In an age conscious of appearance, the wealthy can purchase "beauty," even if the women are not *bunnies* or *sex kittens*, and the men are not *hunks*.

This group of *jet setters* include *WASPs* (white, Anglo-Saxon Protestants), *Jewish Princesses*, and other *upscale trend setters*. The *glitterati* are followed in the press, which also lionizes the *yuppies* who make big salaries in the *meritocracy*.

Minorities

We have already noted the increasing visibility of *minorities* in this period. New names were intended to express a new sense of pride. Negroes referred to themselves as blacks, Indians as *Native Americans*, homosexuals as *gays*. In this survey of terms for people, we find most of the derogatory terms referring to the *mainstream* culture; it is possible that *minorities* actually felt better about themselves than *WASPs* and other *mainstream* people.

Another sexual minority for which the culture struggled to find an appropriate name, was the growing number of *hetero* people who lived together but were not married. "Roommates," "boy friend," and "girl friend," did not *make it*, nor did the terms *old lady* and *old man*, which were unpopular among the largely young people in this category. One attempt which did not make the dictionary was the term "posslq," an acronym from the U.S. census meaning "persons of opposite sex sharing living quarters." The lack of a term for such a widespread phenomenon has been noted occasionally in the press, and would seem to indicate that the *straight* culture was having some trouble accepting this phenomenon.

Summary

The new words naming people serve as a kind of map to the culture's areas of concern and types of value. We see only two kinds of people receiving admiration or respect—powerful *honchos* and *beautiful people*—yet even this respect is admixed with fear or envy. We see *minorities* of all sorts—ethnic and sexual—gaining access to the established language, which is surely a gain for the culture as a whole.

But most visible are the terms of denunciation, which abound for incompetence or stupidity. Next most visible are the mutually denouncing vocabularies of *freaks* and *straights*. Here we see the residue in words of many experiences of frustration and anger, the polarization of society into hostile camps, and the seeds of *miscommunication* on all levels.

Does this crop of new terms indicate a dehumanization of the culture during the 1961–1986 period? A tendency to stereotype people with uncomplimentary labels? On balance, the answer seems to be yes. Yet there is also a hopeful side to this phenomenon, for at least the language is recognizing more types of people and points of view than it did in the past. It will be a challenge to the culture to get beyond the stereotypes of its language and discover the common humanity underlying the diverse appearances.

CHAPTER SEVEN

New Words from Communication

Few New Communication Terms

Communication terms make up one of the smallest groupings in the content analysis of *12,000 Words*, comprising only about 2.4 percent of the total. (See Table 6.)

The relative paucity of new words indicates that the culture was not successfully conceptualizing its communication in new and fruitful ways. It is possible to claim that communication did not change much during the period of study, and therefore required little effort to conceptualize new words. But this is extremely implausible, given the changes in the rest of the culture, and the increased interest in communication during this period. A more likely thesis is that the changes in the outer environment took up so much attention that equally important changes in communication lagged behind in conceptualization.

Table 6. *COMMUNICATION TERMS*

Overall Rank	No. Words	Category	% Words
17	83	Language, Comm. Theory	1.552
23-tie	45	Communication Situations	0.841
TOTAL	128		2.393

Our period saw the increased *politicization* of everyday life, and the emergence of a batch of terms for denouncing others, as discussed in the last chapter. Therefore it is not surprising that when we turn to terms describing communication, we should find a large vocabulary of criticism, attack, and defense developed, while there is a relatively meager set of terms for honest, open communication.

We also see the reflection of a technological society in the strangely impersonal new terms for relationships, as people talk about *hooking up with* each other and *bonding*. In a later section in this chapter, we will discuss the vocabulary of *hype* and performance which seems so prevalent in the culture. Finally we will discuss the metaphors underlying the new speech act verbs and nouns and adjectives for talk.

Critical and Hostile Communication

In this period, we find a rich harvest of words describing varieties of critical or hostile communication. Several main themes can be found in the definitions of the term *shoot down*. Originally referring to the physical act of shooting down balloons or airplanes, in our period the term was metaphorically extended into the communicative realm. *Shoot down* can mean

—to put an end to, defeat; as, shooting down a proposed bill in the legislature;
—to deflate or ridicule; as, to shoot down his request for a date; or
—to discredit by exposing weakness or inaccuracy; as, shooting down a theory.

Note that this little phrase suggests a state of war, and ample verbal armaments for putting an end to any attempted flight of fancy, theory, or hope.

Getting *flak* (abusive criticism) is another term which participates in this metaphor; in World War II, *flak* was a slang term for antiaircraft fire.

You never know when you'll be *under the gun*, and someone will *zing* you with pointed criticism. You might get *zapped* at any time. Some people are experts in the art of the *put down* and are not above *psyching you out* by taking a *cheap shot, blindsiding* you, or delivering a *low blow*.

Once you've been *brought down*, it gets easier to *dump on* you and *trash* your ideas with *nit-picking counterexamples*.

Such *one-upping* can be a real hassle, and you have to *hang in there* and not *freak out* as they try to *do a number on* you. Their ideas may be just so much *noise, doublespeak*, really B.S., but they will try to *rub your nose in it*, even if it is a *crock* (insincere, pretentious, misleading talk).

How do you defend yourself? It's obvious you can't *let it all hang out*. You have to *play your cards* carefully. You can't get caught up in their *head trip*. You need to *psych yourself up* and respond to their gamemanship with your own *upmanship*. *Pull out all the stops*. Show you are *underwhelmed* with their *wordsmanship*. *One-up* their *buzz words* with your own *code words* and *in-jokes*. Pile on the *trivia*. *Defocus* the discussion.

Attack with your own *bafflegab* (pretentiously unintelligble language); perhaps *academese*, *bureaucratese*, *computerese*, *educationese*, or *sociologese*. If you're a real *wordsmith*, you might try the argot of *lit-crit* (literary criticism).

In all this, it helps if you can *field* questions extemporaneously, *play it by ear*, and *wing it* when necessary. It's dangerous to *shoot from the hip* (act or speak hastily without consideration of the consequences). It helps to have some *one-liners* and *throwaway lines* as you do your *bit*.

Such are the extremes an *adversarial* culture can drive one to. We might note here that there is an additional group of terms for hostile and critical communication which apply to game-playing executives described under "executalk" in Chapter 5.

This rich crop of terms describing critical, hostile, or defensive communication situations indicates that the culture has paid much attention to them, as would be expected in the politicized environment. By contrast, we find relatively few terms for open, honest communication.

Honest Communication

One is immediately struck by the paucity of terms for honest communication which American culture has produced during the 1961–1986 time period. Not only the scarcity, but the limited range and fragility of these words becomes apparent on examination.

We can, for instance, *tune in* to someone else. But this media metaphor implies more of a passive receiving role than a participatory one. It also implies that it will be just as easy to *tune out*. A similar passivity can be found in the communicative senses of the terms *turn on* (to interest in) and *turn off* (to withdraw). In all of these, communicating with people is something like switching an appliance on or off.

In relationships, it is ostensibly desirable to be *up front*, to *let it all hang out*, to be *out front*. These terms imply frankness, honesty, openness, yet they also connote vulnerability. It can be dangerous to *let it all hang out*; you are an easy target to get *shot down, put down, dumped on,* or *fucked over.*

To deal with this, a person should be *righteous* (genuine) or *right on* (exactly correct, or attuned to the times), but these terms carry somewhat of a political baggage. *Right on* implies slogans or arguments more than close interpersonal ties; and it would be hard to relax and *hang loose* with a *righteous* person. You can *rap* with people or have a *buzz session,* but these too connote a public occasion demanding a performance more than communicating personally and honestly.

In a good relationship, you might *groove* together, or sometimes you might really get *cookin'* at a party or dance. But these terms, borrowed from musicians' slang, imply a special occasion and/or a heightened consciousness. Nobody can *groove* or *cook* all day.

The science fiction author Robert Heinlein contributed the word *grok* (profound and intuitive understanding) in his novel *Stranger in a Strange Land* (1961). Although it is an interesting concept, combining physical, sexual, and intuitive contact with a deep meditative experience, the term has not received wide use since the book left the bestseller lists.

In the post-1961 period, the term "communication" itself took on a new definition: personal rapport (*Webster's New Collegiate Dictionary,* 8th Edition, 1973). Yet the illustration of the new usage is informative: "a lack of communication between old and young persons." This implies that the new meaning was noticed mainly by its absence. In fact, the phrase "a lack of communication" has become common in this period, being applied almost routinely to explain phenomena as diverse as divorce, losses in sports, and bankruptcies (Phillipsen, 1985).

Likewise the term *miscommunication* entered the language during this period.

This set of terms indicates that, in our period, the culture as a whole has not been expanding, increasing, and reveling in its awareness of honest communication. This impression is furthered when we turn to the new words for relationships.

Relationships

If we have found few terms for honest communication, and many terms for critical and hostile communication, this would imply that interpersonal reltionships might be in some trouble. Interestingly, the warmest emotions are expressed in terms borrowed from *minorities, psychobabble,* and the drug subcultures. Most of the other terms for relationships take on the clinical detachment of the technological society.

You might get *tight* with someone (a term which can mean close or drunk), and be able to be *laid back* with them. You might *cook* or *groove* together on special occasions, and have a *gas.* If you're lucky you might *get it on* with a friend and *make it.* These terms come from *minorities,* particularly jazz musicians, and further indicate that these groups might have had healthier self-feelings and emotional lives than many in the *mainstream* culture.

Other terms for relationships come from the language of *psychobabble* (a predominantly metaphorical language for expressing one's feelings that resembles the hippie argot of the 1960s and is held to be prevalent especially in California). Forming a relationship is helped along by giving each other *strokes.* (In this period, the term means flattering attention designed to reassure or persuade; but in an older meaning it refers to a life-threatening blood clot.)

To help with the difficult process of *consciousness raising,* people joined *encounter groups* or *T-groups,* and did some structured *role playing* to help in their *bonding.*

You might even discover you are in a *karass* with someone (a word coined by novelist Kurt Vonnegut, Jr., to describe a group of people sharing a common interest, even if they don't know it at first). But there's always the danger people might *cop out* on their obligations, or *fink out* on their friends.

Here we can detect a certain ambivalence about *one-on-one* relationships which is nicely captured in the definitions of this term: it can refer to a *face-to-face* encounter, or, in sports, to a style of guarding an opposing player. Likewise a *match-up* can refer to a partnership or a competitive contest.

Many of the terms for relationships take on a sterile quality, a mood of scientific detachment appears. For example, the term *bonding,* or forming a *pair-bond,* sounds as much like chemicals or superglue as people in love.

People seem to find it desirable to do *networking,* where they can just *touch base* occasionally and *interface* (which can be done with a person or a computer). Perhaps through this *inter-individual* contact they can *hook up with* new people and *plug into* a good *thing.* This way they can get the benefits of *groupthink* and *coadapt* to new situations.

Since relationships are becoming so tricky, we find attention directed toward trying to decode the little signs people give off in their *body language*, or their use of *eye contact*, which might *clue us in* to how they really feel. Such *para-language*, when allied with *proxemics* (the study of spatial interactions) is apparently necessary to supplement the meager information coming through verbal channels. You have to keep your *antenna* out to feel the *vibes*.

Performance and Hype

In a communication environment of impersonal relationships, much gamesmanship and little *up-front grokking*, a theme that emerges is the necessity to perform, even in situations which were formerly intimate and private. Even in your personal life, it becomes necessary to practice more *hype*.

People *hype* themselves in interpersonal relationships by *coming on* strong (projecting an image) and trying to *hook* or *grab* others. They try to *hype* their *sexiness*: a generalized term meaning attractiveness or interest. All the gamesmanship, subtle or otherwise, discussed in an earlier section, is also a variety of *hype*.

Of course, advertising and media have developed an entire culture of *hype*, inundating us with widely publicized *non-events* and *media events* which would not exist without it. This culture produced the word *fantabulous*, a combination of fantastic and fabulous, because it was running out of superlatives with which to further *hype* products.

Like so many terms which have come into the respectable language, *hype* originated in a drug subculture. In the 1961 *Unabridged* it was labeled slang, and defined as a hypodermic needle or a narcotics addict. By 1973, in the 8th Edition of *Webster's New Collegiate Dictionary*, however, more definitions were added:

—a deception, put-on (to hype someone);
—extravagent promotion (to hype a performer or show); and
—to stimulate, enliven, increase (to hype sales by gimmicks).

"Hypo" may have been a specialized term in advertising as far back as the 1920s, but it has entered *mainstream* language as *hype*.

Hype as deception can be subtle, as when you *massage* someone's ego through flattery. Or it can involve *massaging* some data to get the right results. Either way, you get *points*, or *brownie points*. As long as no one *blows your cover*, you can continue the *put-on* and *do a number* on anyone.

Minorities have their own words for *hype*, as they *shuck* and *jive Mr. Charlie* with *all that jazz*.

We will see more of the consequences of living in a culture of performance and *hype* in the next section.

Words About Words

To get a closer look at changes in communication during the 1961–1986 period, this section will go beyond the regular content analysis, which forms the basis for structuring this book, and search out terms which specifically refer to talk. The author went through the entire *12,000 Words* dictionary, and located three types of terms: speech act verbs, and nouns and adjectives describing talk.

This procedure has advantages and disadvantages. On the plus side, we are able to get a closer look at an interesting set of terms. On the minus side, this was a one-person content analysis, which is not as reliable as the procedure used in the larger analyses. These issues are discussed further in Appendix 2.

My search found 74 speech act verbs, and 90 nouns and adjectives describing talk, a total of 164 words out of approximately 12,000.

These words were then divided into positive, neutral, or negative categories. A word was coded positive if it implied that open communication was occurring, information was increasing, and/or positive emotions occurred. A word was coded negative if it implied that deception or inaccurate communication was occurring, information was decreasing, and/or negative emotions occurred. Neutral terms carried no particular connotation. Some terms could be both positive or negative, and were coded +/−.

Speech Act Verbs

Speech act verbs, according to the sociolinguist Anna Wierzbicka (1986), are a "valuable source of insight into the culture associated with that language." The names of the repertoire of speech acts encode a culture's view of its most relevant forms of talk. The 74 speech act verbs (with 3 rated both + and −) are shown in Table 7.

Table 7. *NEW SPEECH ACT VERBS*

Neutral (9)

anchor	field	play by ear
call in sick	go	posit
call on	interview	wing it

Positive (25)

blow away (+/−)	hook up	pull one's coat
blow one's mind (+/−)	interface	rap
cool it	let it all hang out	role-play
come out	massage	shoot from the hip (+/−)
free-associate	pick up on	sign on
go public	play the dozens	stroke
grab	plug into	touch base
groove	psych up	turn on
hang lose		

Negative (43)

bad-mouth	hang in there	put the make on
blindside	hang tough	put the screws on
blow away (+/−)	hassle	rub one's nose in it
blow one's cool	hype	scam
blow one's cover	jawbone	send up
blow one's mind (+/−)	kvetch	shoot from hip (+/−)
choke	lean on	shoot down
come on	lowball	shuck
cop out	one-up	stick it to
do a number on	overrespond	stonewall
downplay	play games	trash
dump on	poor-mouth	turn off
fink out	psych out	waffle
freak out	put down	zap
		zing

Over half the new speech act verbs fall into the negative category (55.84 percent). About one-third are positive (32.46 percent), and one-tenth neutral (11.68 percent). This indicates that changes in communication were predominantly negative during the 1961–1986 period—at least this is a hypothesis which can be applied to other samplings of the cultural conversation.

These speech act verbs were further analyzed by searching out their underlying metaphors. Much, if not all, of our languge is metaphorical, and the power of metaphor allows us to understand the new in terms of the familiar (see Lakoff and Johnson, 1980). The author was able to group the terms into semantic fields, with an underlying metaphor, theme, or common discourse of origin.

Looking at the negative speech act verbs, we find the underlying metaphor of DECEPTION-MYSTIFICATION in 10 terms:

come on	play games
do a number on	poor-mouth
downplay	psych out
hype	scam
lowball	stonewall

The metaphor of COMBAT-WAR underlay nine terms:

blow away	stick it to
blow one's cover	trash
overrespond	zap
shoot down	zing
shoot from the hip	

The theme of SOCIAL PRESSURE underlay eight terms:

blow one's cool	lean on
hassle	put the make on
jawbone	put the screws on
kvetch	waffle

The theme of COMPETITION underlay eight terms:

badmouth	one-up
blindside	put down
choke	rub one's nose in it
dump on	send-up

Other metaphorical areas are DRUG EXPERIENCES (three terms: *blow one's mind, freak out, turn off*) and the theme of UNFAITHFULNESS (two terms: *fink out, cop out*).

When we turn to the emotionally neutral terms, one coherent semantic field could be labeled IMPROMPTU PERFORMANCES:

field	play by ear
go	wing it

Another field of neutral terms might be called DEALING WITH AUTHORITY:

call in sick	interview
call on	posit

Coming to the positive speech act verbs, the largest group of terms (nine) comes from the therapeutic languge disparagingly called PSYCHOBABBLE:

free-associate	pick up on
grab	psych up
hang loose	role-play
let it all hang out	stroke
massage	

The second largest group of positive terms (six) comes from MINORITY groups of different sorts (blacks, sexual minorities):

come out	play the dozens
cool it	pull one's coat
groove	rap

The third largest group of positive speech act verbs (five) comes from DRUG EXPERIENCES:

blow away	groove
blow one's mind	turn on
cool it	

(In this list, *cool it* and *groove* also come from *minorities*.)

The fourth largest group of terms (four) has an underlying TECHNOLOGICAL metaphor:

hook up   plug into
interface   turn on (also in
                            drugs)

We also find a COMPETITION theme in *shoot from the hip,* and *psych up.* SOCIAL PRESSURE is implied by *go public.*

This listing of underlying metaphors and themes for new speech act verbs gives us a look at the deep structure of the discourse about discourse.

The semantic fields describe a cultural situation where the most attention is paid to communication which is deceptive, combative, harshly competitive, and carrying social pressure (the negative terms).

In this situation, you need skills to improvise, *play it by ear,* and deal with authority (the neutral terms).

In this harsh environment, therapy or therapeutic situations are required to express positive emotions to others, release is sought in drugs or drug-like experiences, and it is often wise to approach people in an impersonal, technological manner (the positive terms). Interestingly enough, *minority* speech provides several positive communication terms, implying that more positive speech acts occurred among *minorities* than in the *mainstream.*

This picture of a harsh communication environment is consistent with the politicized society we find described by the other new words. If communication was becoming so unpleasant, perhaps it is less surprising to find relatively few new words describing it.

The results of the analysis of speech act verbs are further confirmed by the study of nouns and adjectives describing talk, to be discussed in the next section.

Nouns and Adjectives for Talk

The author found 90 nouns and adjectives describing talk. Coding them into positive, neutral, and negative categories produced 47 negative, 27 positive, and 21 neutral terms (5 terms were double-coded $+/-$, possibly having either connotation). These are listed in Table 8.

The percentage of terms in the negative category is 49.47 percent, or approximately half, which is similar to the percentage for speech act verbs. Positive terms made up 28.4 percent, roughly one-third,

Table 8. *NEW NOUNS AND ADJECTIVES FOR TALK*

Neutral (21)

acrolect	franglais	sprechstimme
arabesque	japlish	spritz
basilect	instruction (computer)	statement (computer)
bit	language (machine)	tag question
catechism	megillah	talking head
code-switching	schtick	throwaway
conversation	spanglish	yinglish
(w/computer)		

Positive (27)

bag	laid back	righteous
buzz session	networking	show & tell (+/−)
chutzpah (+/−)	one-liner	sign
consciousness-raising	one-on-one (+/−)	signifying
cued speech	out-front	talk show
drumbeat	oral history	rib tickler
head trip (+/−)	pas de deux (+/−)	teach-in
interactive (system)	pillow talk	up-front
interface	rap	(a) yuck

Negative (47)

academese	educationese	put-down
arm-twisting	face-off	put-on
ass-kissing	flak	scam
bafflegab	hard-line	shoot-out
bleep	head trip (+/−)	show & tell (+/−)
bop	in-joke	slurvian
BS	jive	snake oil
bureaucratese	low blow	sociologese
buzz word	needle	static
cheap shot	newspeak	sting
chutzpah (+/−)	nit-picking	swipe
code-word	noise	tic
computerese	nonfluency	toe-to-toe
cop-out	one-on-one (+/−)	upmanship
crock	pas de deux (+/−)	zinger
doublespeak	psychobabble	

which is also similar to the verbs. And neutral terms made up 22.1 percent, slightly higher than the verbs.

The underlying semantic fields for the nouns and adjectives relating to talk are very similar to those for the speech act verbs.

The top negative category is DECEPTION-MYSTIFICATION, with 18 terms:

academese	doublespeak
bafflegab	educationese
bop	jive
BS	newspeak
bureaucratese	noise
buzz word	put-on
code word	snake oil
computerese	sociologese
crock	sting

The next category is COMPETITION, with 14 terms:

cheap shot	one-on-one
chutzpah	put-down
face-off	static
in-joke	swipe
low blow	toe-to-toe
needle	upmanship
nit-picking	zinger

SOCIAL PRESSURE has three terms:

arm-twisting	show & tell
ass-kissing	

COMBAT-WAR also has three terms:

flak	shootout
hard-line	

PSYCHOBABBLE is itself a new term, and includes itself and *head trip*, which might also be classified as a DRUG EXPERIENCE.

The neutral terms again show a large IMPROMPTU PERFORMANCE set of terms (9):

bit	schtick
catechism	sprechstimme
code-switching	spritz
megillah	tag question
	throwaway

In addition, neutral terms include TECHNOLOGICAL terms for communication with computers (four):

conversation	language
instruction	statement

The blending of English and other languages produces four terms:

franglais	spanglish
japlish	yinglish

The positive category again shows PSYCHOBABBLE with the largest number of terms (8):

bag	laid back
buzz session	out-front
consciousness raising	righteous
head trip	up-front

MINORITY terms include terms from the black ghetto game signifying, and two deaf terms:

cued speech	sign
rap	signifying

COMEDY terms include:

one-liner	(a)yuck
rib-tickler	

Positive TECHNOLOGICAL terms include:

interactive	networking
interface	

Two terms from LOVERS are:

pillow talk	pas de deux

This analysis of nouns and adjectives for talk reinforces the conclusions from the earlier study of speech act verbs. During our period, talk, language, communication became increasingly deceptive, competitive, and combative. To cope, one needed to improvise. Positive emotion needed a therapeutic or *counterculture* milieu to be expressed.

CHAPTER EIGHT

New Words for Psychological States

A Map of Inner States

Our tour of the city of words ends with a section of the map not visible on ordinary maps of ordinary cities. For new words form a map, not only of changes in outer experience, but of changed inner states as well.

In the politicized and hypercritical world that was emerging, serious inner changes occurred. The new words tell us that a coherent identity became harder to maintain, as more stress was put on performances for the moment. This performing self is highlighted by the new terms of the period.

The categories of psychological terms form the smallest grouping in the content analysis, 1.15 percent of the total words (see Table 9). This lack of new terms for inner states indicates a culture that is putting most of its attention toward the outer world—extroverted and other-directed. As with communication terms, psychological terms lag behind new words for "things" in the outer environment.

Table 9. *PSYCHOLOGY TERMS*

Overall Rank	No. of Words	Category	% Words
23-tie	45	Psychological Theory	0.841
35	17	Psychological States	0.317
TOTAL	62		1.158

To see the changes in *personhood* more clearly, the next sections will, in addition to constructing mini-narratives from new words, also trace changes in dictionary definitions of certain terms which have remained in use, but which have changed meanings. In particular, new definitions of "identity," "identification," "identity crisis," "anxiety," "performance," and "guilt" will be noted.

The Self in Crisis

One narrative that can be constructed from the new terms in this period shows a "self" that is increasingly being formed by "identification" with outside people. Thus the important issues to this "other-directed self" focus around issues related to performance and self-control. It is especially important to keep control over your appearances by keeping *cool*, dealing with backstage anxiety, controlling your anger, and dealing with depression. What about happiness? The new terms indicate happiness comes in short *flashes*. Relaxation seems difficult to come by, and there is much concern with the ultimate loss of control, craziness.

The new phrase, "looking out for *numero uno*" leaves little doubt of the place of the self in American thinking.

Yet the very wideness of the use of the term "self" hides a significant shift in our sense of ourselves which occurs during our period. This shift has been observed many times, but was formulated in the 1950s by two sociologists who will be taken as, indeed, prophets of the culture to come.

David Reisman (1953) wrote that the personality structure of Americans was changing from an inner-directed type (guided by a firm set of internal standards) to an other-directed type (tending to conform to shifting group norms).

Erving Goffman (1959) developed a sociology of performance as accounting for the *Presentation of Self in Everyday Life*. In the performance, it was the appearance of the moment that counted—a stable sense of self could be dispensed with.

Other authors have noted these shifts, in varying vocabularies. Professor Howard Gadlin (1984) sums up much of the literature in the observation that "(t)oday, in psychiatric establishments, we assume a degree of fragmentation in personal style which, in the past, would be indicative of pathology."

While some authors have seen this shift as evidence of cultural decline (see Lasch, 1979), others such as Robert Lifton (1971) took a more positive approach. In his essay "Protean Man," Lifton celebrated the many-sided potentials of the new, diffuse character structure, and seemed relatively untroubled by its lack of continuity.

In popular terminology, this new diffuseness is summarized nicely in the term *together*. It applies to one person, not two or more, and means composed in mind or manner, or prepared, organized, balanced. It implies that a person might fly apart without the effort to get it all *together*.

If you don't *clean up your act* and get it *together*, you might feel *schizy* when the gaps between your different performing selves becomes too great.

This is the period when the term *identity crisis* enters the language. Coined in the 1950s by the psychiatrist Erik Erikson, it appears in *6,000 Words* (Merriam-Webster, 1976) as:

> psychosocial conflict or confusion in an individual concerning his social role that may be accompanied by loss of feelings of sameness and continuity of the personality and that occurs especially during adolescence in response to changes in internal drives and to external pressures to adopt new roles.

The above definition was repeated in *9,000 Words* (Merriam-Webster, 1983a), with the following addition:

> broadly: a similar state of confusion in an institution or organization.

Clearly, *identity crises* were not just for adolescents anymore. *12,000 Words* (Merriam-Webster, 1986) rewords these definitions yet again but does not change their substance.

It is interesting that we do not find a set of new terms to describe the stages of the *identity crisis* or the means for its triumphant resolution. On these the language is silent. Instead what we find, in *12,000 Words*, is the *mid-life crisis* (a period of emotional turmoil in middle age caused by the realization that one is no longer young and characterized especially by a strong desire for change). This suggests that the *identity crisis* has not been solved so much as postponed.

Identity from Identification

And what of this identity which was in crisis? We can trace the changes toward an other-directed identity by comparing definitions in different editions of the *Collegiate Dictionaries* during the 1961–1986 period.

"Identity" in its generic sense has always meant sameness through different circumstances. The specific applications of the term to personal identity interest us here. In both the 6th Edition

(Merriam-Webster, 1949) and the 7th Edition (Merriam-Webster, 1963) we find identity defined as:

> 2. Unity and persistence of personality.

This definition is gone in 1973, replaced by:

> 2a. The distinguishing character or personality of an individual: Individuality.

Note the shift from an inner-directed definition (unity and persistence) to one that focuses on uniqueness in performance (distinguishing character). A second definition appears in 1973:

> 2b. The relation established by psychological identification.

This leads us to consider the process of "psychological identification," which has come to be important in the establishing of identity.

In the 7th Edition (Merriam-Webster, 1963), a new definition of the term "identification" appears:

> 2. Orientation of the self in regard to something (as a person or a group) with a resulting feeling of close personal association.

In 1973 (8th Edition), this new definition is added:

> 2b. A mental mechanism whereby the individual attains gratification, emotional support, or relief from stress by consciously or unconsciously attributing to himself the characteristics of another person or a particular group.

This newest definition is changed in 1983 (9th Edition) to:

> 2b. A largely unconscious process whereby an individual models thoughts, feelings, and actions after those attributed to an object that has been incorporated as a mental image.

The struggle to define the processes of identification indicates a fluid term, one that is still the subject of interest and debate. Significantly for our narrative, it reflects the rise of the other-directed person, the person who turns outside him/herself for clues about who to be. Is the process largely conscious or unconscious? The definitions are not definitive, although by 1983 the balance was tilted toward unconsciousness.

These terms trace what has happened to the "self" during our period. True, the old terms "personality" and "self" persist through the period. We can not contend that all sense of a coherent self has disappeared. The linguistic evidence does indicate that more attention is being paid to the notion of an other-directed self.

Indeed, the center seems to give way quietly, almost unnoticed in the distractions and complexities of the performances demanded by the new society. A new identity-formation of other-directedness is described by the emergent new vocabulary. This vocabulary centers on issues of performance and self-control, not coherence and self-consistency.

Performing and Keeping Cool

The other-directed identity cannot fall back on inner guiding principles; instead it must look for cues from outside. Action takes on the nature of a performance, and it becomes more important to keep up appearances than perhaps ever before. It is interesting to trace some differences in the word "performance" during our period.

In 1949, performance meant the execution of required functions (a motor could deliver a performance), or a presentation of a play or other public exhibition of skill.

By 1963 the definition had been added:

5. the manner of reacting to stimulii: behavior.

In 1983, another definition was added:

6. linguistic behavior—compare competence.

(Linguistic competence refers to the knowledge required to speak and understand a language, performance refers to the act of speaking, etc.).

We may take this expansion of the use of "performance" as a corroboration of Erving Goffman's sociology of performance detailed in *The Presentation of Self in Everyday Life* (1959). All behavior, and particularly linguistic behavior, starts to be defined as performance.

In a performance situation, you must keep your self-control. The issue of control over appearances becomes very important to the other-directed personality, if our listing of new terms in the language is an accurate guide. You may have to *clean up your act* so you can *cut it* with the people you're trying to impress and *come off* the way you want to.

You need to be *cool*, to *cool it*, not *blow your cool*, or be *uncool*. These terms, from the slang of jazz musicians and beats in the 1950s, entered general use in the 1960s, and meant "to keep or regain control of one's emotions."

If you are *cool*, you can *hang in there* and not *freak out* if someone lays a *head trip* on you. If you *blow your cool*, you might *choke* (lose your composure and fail to perform effectively in a critical situation). You might make a "Freudian slip," which would reveal more than you wanted to. Or worse, you might *flip out* (lose self-control) and come *unglued* (being in a confused or agitated state).

Much better to be *unflappable* (marked by assurance and self-control) than *flappable, hip,* than *unhip,* show *couth* rather than uncouth. You've got to keep *dry-eyed* and you can't look *uptight*. No matter how they might try, don't let them *blow your cover*.

Note the mixture of performance and self-control in the new terminology. This implies that not only Goffmann, but Kenneth Burke, with his metaphor of social process as drama, were appropriate prophets of the new culture.

Anxiety

Keeping up appearances, however, takes psychological energy. Backstage, there is a good deal of anxiety. We will look at the new terms *psych* and *psych-out*, for an insight into this situation.

If you *psych* yourself, you get psychologically ready for performance. If you *psych* someone else, you try to intimidate them, or *psych them out*. In *9,000 Words* (1983) we find the following example of a *psych-out*: you always make a show of confidence, while you work to undermine the confidence of your opposition.

The term *psych*, of course, is short for psychology, which implies that you need to *do a number on* your own total mind-set, in order to perform in the competitive society.

To *psych* yourself, it helps to have *machismo*, to be able to act *ballsy* (aggressively tough, gutsy). You can't let your *hang-ups* get in the way. You need *chutzpah* (a Yiddish term meaning supreme self-confidence, nerve, gall). You need to get yourself *up, stoked, wired,* so you can *come on* strong.

In matters of performance, however, you must be careful not to look like you're on an *ego-trip,* or like you're *playing games* (hiding the truth by deceptive means). Therefore, much of the backstage *psyching up* to *psych out* others must remain private and hidden— probably one reason the culture has produced few new words for honest, open communication; and many for critical and hostile communication.

We get a further glimpse backstage, at the anxiety of a culture of performance, by tracing changes in the definitions of "anxiety" in the *Collegiate Dictionaries.*

In 1963, the 7th Edition, "anxiety" is defined as:

1a. Painful or apprehensive uneasiness of mind usually over an impending or anticipated ill;
1b. Solicitous concern or interest;
2. A cause of anxiety.

These older definitions are retained in 1973 (8th Edition), but there is an additional definition:

2. An abnormal and overwhelming sense of apprehension and fear, often marked by physiological signs (as sweating, tension, and increased pulse), by doubt concerning the reality and nature of the threat, and by self-doubt about one's capacity to cope with it.

This definition points out the shadowy nature of the causes of anxiety (doubt concerning the reality. . . of the threat) and the persistent self-doubts that come into focus with the other-directed personality.

Guilt

In the classic inner-directed personality, a major source of anxiety was guilt, from an active (perhaps overactive) conscience. Some observers have claimed that the new other-directed personality does not feel guilt in the same way, and may lack a conscience or superego altogether (Lifton, 1971; Lasch, 1979).

We can find some support for this position by noting a new definition of "guilt" in the 1973 edition of the *Collegiate Dictionary:*

2b. feelings of culpability, especially for imagined offenses or from a sense of inadequacy.

Lifton (1971) notes the sense of inadequacy of "Protean Man"—the inability to fulfill all the potentials that seem so near. He sees it as the emotion which has replaced guilt in the old inner-directed identity. We can also note here the struggling with imagined offenses which also appear in the new definitions for anxiety. In a performance culture, it seems to be getting harder to distinguish what "really" is happening.

Anger

With such an emphasis on keeping up a front, with accompanying anxiety, not surprisingly, anger must be kept under control. Many of the new terms for anger tend to minimize it.

One doesn't get angry, one gets *ticked*, or *ticked off*; or maybe *pissed*, or *pissed off*. None of these terms implies rage or even a deep anger. Even if you're *pissed*, you probably won't do much about it other than *kvetch*.

More serious is getting *bent out of shape*, or being *up the wall*. These imply that you are reaching the limits of your endurance.

What might you do then? You might *hassle* someone (subject them to persistent or acute annoyance: harass them). Or you might try to *fuck* them *over*. You might even get physical and *punch* them *out*.

If you get into really extreme situations, you might *off* them, *waste* them, *ice* them, *rub* them *out*, *blow them away*, with your *Saturday Night Special*.

This minute coding of different degrees of anger indicates that the culture has paid a good deal of attention to the subject, and can distinguish between different gradations with some subtlety. The same can not be said for happiness, which we will discuss in the next section.

Happiness

A look at new definitions for the term "happy" in the *Collegiate Dictionaries* is not encouraging. In 1963 (7th Edition), the term "punch happy" appeared (characterized by a dazed, irresponsible state). In 1973 (8th Edition), "enthusiastic to the point of obsession: statistic-happy" appeared.

To indicate that American culture was not completely without happiness in these years, we will all be relieved to note another new definition of happiness appearing in 1973: "having or marked by an atmosphere of good fellowship: friendly."

When we turn to the new words themselves, we find a mixture of drug-related terms and hot and violent metaphors.

If a party is a real *turn-on*, we can *get off* and have a *blast*. It's *kicky* to watch people *go ape* and see all their *freakiness*.

Of course, you can get *mellow* and *laid back*, and *groove* until you *bliss out* on *cloud nine*. But if you're really *flying*, you can feel the *rush*, get a *flash*, and be totally *bombed*.

These terms do not describe sustained, pleasant, glowing happiness. Instead we get drug-aided states, usually in short, intense *flashes*. Not only can anger become explosive, but happiness also.

We may note here that the new term *crack up* (to laugh out loud, or cause to laugh out loud), in older meanings referred to going crazy, or having an automobile crash. Loss of control, craziness, and laughter are all joined together in this semantic clustering. Once again we see the need for control in a performance culture.

Depression

All this need for control can get to be depressing. Some days you might have the *blahs* (a feeling of boredom, discomfort, and general dissatisfaction). Life generally is a *drag*. You worry about your *self-worth*. You don't want to become a *basket case*. Should you go to a *shrink*?

In such situations, Americans have increasingly turned to drugs—legal and illegal—for an *upper*. This association of drugs and depression is found in a number of terms. If you are depressed, you feel life is a *bummer*, or a *downer*. These two terms originally described bad drug *trips*. The energy-draining aftermath of such experiences has given rise to a number of words which also apply to both areas. You can be *spaced out*, *strung out*, *zonked*, *wasted*, *whacked-out*, or *wrecked*.

This confluence of drug and depression-related terms implies that the two experiences have fed upon each other. Once again we see the terms from a subculture being called upon to graphically describe a situation in the *mainstream* culture; implying that there is some similarity in the respective experiences.

Relaxation

In a culture of performance and *flashes* of happiness, there is a constant danger of *burnout*, and it seems to be a rare occasion when one can get *mellow* and *laid back* (easygoing, unhurried). We have few new words describing such experiences. Interestingly enough, a German word was imported for describing a mood of cordiality, friendliness: *gemutlichkeit*.

Specific methods of relaxation did gain attention during this period, such as *Transcendental Meditation* and other forms of meditation, and physical means of releasing tension like *rolfing, tai chi,* or *tae kwan do*. Some people went into early memories in *primal scream therapy*. Technology got into the act with *biofeedback* machines which told you when your brainwaves were in *alpha* rhythms. *Endorphins* were discovered (naturally occurring proteins in the brain which produce feelings of well-being).

However, the lack of new words describing relaxed states indicates that perhaps the culture spent more time seeking relaxation than finding it.

Craziness

The culture has definitely been concerned with craziness during the 1961–1986 period. We find a range of terms, from *borderline* to *bonkers*, to describe degrees of craziness.

"Crazy" becomes a noun for the first time. A *crazy*, or a group of *crazies*, refers to "one who is or acts crazy, especially such a one associated with a radical or extremist political cause" (Merriam-Webster, 1986). This is *fallout* from the mutually denouncing vocabularies of *straights* and *freaks* discussed in Chapter 4. A *crazy* is, however, usually conceived as a long-haired *freak*, not as a technocrat with a tie calculating *megadeaths*.

Some people are just *borderline*, while others are *kooky*, which is still not too bad. Such a person may go to a *psychoquack* who talks *psychobabble* and is a little *wiggy* themselves. If people act *wacko* it still may be amusing, for they are probably just *out to lunch*.

But if you start to *hallucinate* imaginary companions, or have *flashbacks*, you could really go *bananas* or *bonkers*. This is worse than being *schizy*, you are a "schizo" (first appearing in the 1963 *Seventh*

New Collegiate Dictionary). Then you are a candidate for the *funny farm*.

Craziness is, of course, the ultimate loss of control over your performances. Perhaps that is why there exists this finely graded set of distinctions in the new terms. The other-directed self can only know it is sane if it is performing in a controlled manner.

CHAPTER NINE

Words as Predictors

Language as Reality-Constructor

Our tour of the city of words, or at least of its new additions in the quarter century from 1961 to 1986, is over. The new words of the time have mapped out changes in experience, and told us stories of a culture becoming more complex, contentious, and confusing.

It is now time to shift metaphors in our treatment of new words. The map metaphor has been useful for descriptive purposes, but it is static in nature. Language does not stand still, as the new words themselves illustrate. We may freeze our talk (la parole) into printed words on a page, but we must not forget that our spoken words are active parts of our lives. They are doing a job. To shift metaphors, words are tools.

What do we use the tools of language to do? In one influential view, we use our conversation to construct and maintain an interpreted reality (Berger and Luckmann, 1966).

We inhabit an interpreted world, and we get quite uncomfortable when our interpretations do not fit our experience. Thus we spend a good deal of time and effort to maintain, repair, or revise our definitions of reality (Mehan and Wood, 1975).

Our conversation, then, can be seen as an apparatus for the construction and maintenance of definitions of reality. In this metaphorical view, language does more than passively map reality, it participates in shaping and constructing our reality. (See Carey, 1975; Pearce and Cronen, 1980.) For we use words to think with, to carve shapes in experience, to rope in ephemeral patterns and communicate about them. The words we use will influence, to some degree, the thoughts we can have and the conclusions we can draw. The words we use will influence what we can and cannot communicate.

We may ask, then, what realities can be constructed with our new words? What kind of social reality will they contribute to shaping? Looking at the new tools in our vocabulary, what predictions can we make about their future products?

Predicting Social Realities

If the trends in the vocabulary continue, we can predict a social reality of increasing stereotypes, ideology, and social conflict.

As our dependence on *high tech* continues, we will live with the peculiar mixture of helplessness and power that we have called the "techno-trap."

As *hardball*-playing business managers face the increasing complexities of the world economy, business will become less socially responsible, in the ruthless scramble for the *bottom line*.

We will routinely get *doublespeak* in our communication, and we will increasingly define communication in combative terms.

As the social environment becomes more harsh, and the economic environment more ruthless, people will become more *schizy*. More effort will go into performances, simulating and dissimulating.

As people become less reliable, more emphasis will be placed on therapies of all sorts. Also, security will be sought in machines. An anthropomorphizing of machinery, already well-developed with computers, will make people seem more like inferior machines, and less like human beings. This will produce a human *identity crisis*, to be discussed later.

The basis for these predictions will become clear if we review the new words in each of our categories. Since communication is so central in the reality-construction process, we will begin our review with the terms from communication.

Overview of the Narratives as a Whole

The discourse describing communication relies heavily on metaphors of competition, combat, deception, and mystification. The culture paid most attention to gamesmanship, *hype*, and *doublespeak*. The harsh communications environment put a premium on *winging it*, improvising, and playing for the moment.

There is no question that honest communication did occur, and some people were *up front* with each other, but they required a therapeutic or *counterculture* vocabulary to *let it all hang out*.

Since the self is constructed in a social conversation, when that conversation becomes unclear, critical, and downright hostile, the self must react with defensive calculations. In this environment, those who try to stick to a firm set of internal standards suffer from stresses that occasionally lead to an *identity crisis*. Instead, it proves more rewarding to "identify" with others, and perform as the moment seems to require.

The theme of performance appears throughout the new words in the 1961–1986 period. *Hardball*-playing executives need to know the *name of the game* to perform properly. *Turkeys* and other *screw-ups* are denounced because they can't perform. If you keep your *cool*, you'll be able to perform and not *choke*.

However, with the growing *politicization* of everyday life, you may have to perform with *straights* one minute and with *freaks* the next. You may have to agree with *environmentalist* values even as you drink from a *throwaway* container. You may use your *word processor* to write a treatise attacking computers. Such *mind-blowing* situations can lead to a sense of being *schizy*, not quite *together*.

So as people *hype* themselves more, there seems to be less actually there to *hype*. *Method acting*, popularized in the 1950s, became a national habit. Anxiety became a constant, free-floating problem which resembled stage fright. People *psych up* for performances so they can *cut it* in the new social environment. Keeping it *together* for the moment takes precedence over discovering basic inner values. This approach to life leads to no resolution of the *identity crisis*, but instead its postponement into a *mid-life crisis*.

Meantime the hostile and uncertain communications environment produces a depersonalization of relationships. We *network* with others, *plug into* relationships, get *turned off* or *turned on* by them. These technological images construct a reality much less personal than the older terms do: where we keep in touch with others, share relationships, and get disgusted or delighted with what eventuates.

We also see stereotyping in the mutually denouncing vocabularies of *freaks* and *straights*, the labeling of *turkeys*, *heavies*, and *beautiful people*. Such stereotypes, aided by simplified media representations, pose an increasing barrier to discovering our common humanity, and imply a coming age of increased prejudice, ideology, and social conflict.

And even as we dehumanize people with our language, we humanize machines. This tendency was discovered by motivational researchers in the late 1930s and 1940s, who found that men fantasized about their cars as if they were their mistresses (Dichter, 1960, Appendix 2). Yet the anthropomorphizing vocabulary for computers indicates that this trend is growing. The computer is spoken of as a *brain*, as having a *memory*, which you can *converse* with through a computer *language*.

This humanization of machines, which will be discussed later in this chapter, is but one aspect of the culture's fascination with technology. Terms from Science and Technology make up 45.24 percent of the new words in the *12,000 Words* dictionary. This dwarfs the 3.55 percent of new words from Communication and Psychology, indicating a massive flow of cultural attention outward into the material world of gadgets and things.

The culture is quick to seek the technological *fix* for its problems, but often "second-order effects" appear which are unforeseen and put the applications of the technology into question. This leads to a search for yet another technological *fix*, and a self-perpetuating logic places the society squarely into a "techno-trap"—being dependent upon a technology yet not understanding it nor being able to control its *ripple effects*.

At the same time, the economy has become more confusing, unpredictable, and *counterintuitive*. As the stakes of a world empire have gotten bigger, the strategies to follow have become less clear. Economic theory found itself trying to explain situations like *stagflation* which were not supposed to happen. As a result, a vocabulary of game-playing and the *bottom line* emerged to conceptualize and justify managerial decision making. Sport became a managerial metaphor, as people wondered if the economy could be controlled at all (see MacIntyre, 1981, pp. 71–75).

The newly complex economy and the world-spanning economic empire did produce widespread affluence, more consumer goods, greater variety in lifestyles, more kinds of food available, more travel, vacation, work, and school opportunities. This variety extended to the emergence above ground of formerly taboo sexual and drug subcultures. Women and ethnic minorities became more "visible" as well, politically, economically, and socially. Behavior that used to be "backstage" moved out into the public eye to become very "frontstage."

Yet this variety in lifestyles produced strains and *politicization* in many areas of life. Intolerance of some of the most flagrant differences led to a resurgence of ideologies in an age when ideology had supposedly ended. Many everyday acts became problematic in the incipient *environmentalist* awareness. The language of stereotyping others further reinforced tendencies to depersonalize and ideologize social life.

This overview of the narratives constructed from new words provides a coherent picture of changes in experience in hyper-modern American culture from 1961 to 1986. The picture is not necessarily flattering, and tells a tale we have labeled as ironic. The culture produces great affluence, but also great social division and strife. It develops advanced technologies, but loses its personal identity. It produces tremendous military power, but finds itself a hair-trigger away from destruction.

These stories may be interpreted from a number of different viewpoints—no claim is made here for the exclusivity or primacy of my interpretations. What is interpreted as ironic, for example, may be seen as fatal contradictions. No single interpretation can encompass the richness and diversity of the material provided by our new words. No single interpretation can exhaust the evidence or forestall all criticism.

Yet through this complex and contentious period, the culture still exhibits its creativity, still strives to understand, generating new words and new concepts to codify its new experiences. Yet if the new words are not chosen carefully, they may only exacerbate the problems posed by a technological society. For the language shows a process of externalizing human qualities onto machines, at the same time internalizing mechanical qualities into humans. This will produce a "human *identity crisis*," which can only grow in the future unless language is carefully used. The next section will discuss this problem in more detail.

Computers and the Human Identity Crisis

In this section we will discuss a two-fold process, which is discoverable in our language, although it does not take place solely there, and which we may call the human *identity crisis*. This crisis involves first, the externalization of human qualities onto machines, and second, the internalization of machine qualities into humans. Both are occurring, and both are encouraged by the careless use of language. It makes a difference whether we speak of a computer as having a "memory" or a "data-storage capacity." As a result of this crisis, we have less sense of what is human, less sense of humans as distinct from machines, more sense of powerful machines and frail humans. The crisis will only be made worse by careless use of language; it may be partly solveable by proper use of language.

On the one hand, the metaphorical use of human terms like "memory" for computer capacities is a way of making complex technological functions more understandable. While this is a desirable goal, some serious confusions will arise from this tactic. This author does not believe that computers "think" or have "memories," neither does he believe that humans are machines. Linguistically confusing humans and machines amounts to a serious category mistake, which will only confuse philosophical conversation in the culture.

To begin with the externalization of human qualities onto machines, a brief look at the history of the word "technology" is instructive.

In the nineteenth century and into the twentieth, "technology" had two definitions. In the 3rd Edition of *Webster's Collegiate Dictionary* (Merriam-Webster, 1916), technology was defined as "science or systematic knowledge of the industrial arts;" and it was "the terminology used in arts, sciences, etc."

Interestingly, these definitions reveal that "technology" was in people, it was people's knowledge and language. Today, the "technology" is built into artifacts. We speak of things as being *high-tech*, not people.

The definition of "technology" has also expanded, so by 1963 it was defined as "the totality of the means employed to provide objects necessary for human sustenance and comfort." Here we see an increasingly wide use for the term technology, and at the same time a removal from its location in humans.

This process of externalization of human qualities onto machines can be noted in other terms as well. By 1963, for example, a communications network was defined as a "nerve center." And the findings of motivational research in advertising, for example, the idea that men thought of their first car as their mistress, show the same tendency (Dichter, 1960).

But the most massive externalization of human qualities onto machines is probably yet to come. The first ripples of it can be seen in the computer terms that have already entered the dictionary. A computer is spoken of as a *brain*, and advanced systems have *artificial intelligence*.

Indeed, by 1983, a new definition of "intelligent" was:

3. able to perform computer functions (an intelligent terminal) also able to convert digital information to hard copy (an intelligent copier).

Intelligence is not just for people any more.

As early as 1963 (7th Edition), a new definition of "memory" included "electronic computing machines." By 1973 (8th Edition), certain plastics were held to have "memory" as well.

A new definition of "conversation" in 1973 was: "An exchange similar to conversation, especially real-time interaction with a computer especially through a keyboard."

These conversations could occur because machines were held to have their own "language." *Machine language* appeared in the 1973 *Collegiate Dictionary*, along with *machine-readable* (directly usable by a computer). In fact, "language" itself took on a new definition as early as 1963 which referred to computer operations. Because the machine could read language, it is not surprising to see computer information described as *words*.

This linguistic externalization of human qualities onto computers will probably only be intensified as *robots* come into more prominence. But this projection of mind into machines is already serious. For although language does not determine thought, it can influence habits of thinking which shape our world-view in important ways (Whorf, 1956). Any discussions of computers—or humans, for that matter—using the anthropomorphized vocabulary above will be subtly pressured toward certain conclusions.

Do computers think? Do they have rights? Are they conscious? Such questions are being discussed, and the language in which they are discussed can be crucial. If the computer is held to have a *memory*, and the ability to *read words* and translate them into its own *language*, thereby to make *intelligent* choices, the very terms themselves will dictate a conclusion that computers are conscious, thinking beings, with attendant rights and responsibilities.

But if we say that computers have data storage capacities (instead of "memory"), that they can *input* and scan information in their own codes and perform mathematical choice-functions, then the conclusion will be biased in another way, toward a more mechanical view that computers do not really think, and are not really conscious in the human sense.

Here is a case where real confusions can result in our thinking from the language we use. And we have a choice in this matter; we do not need to use anthropormorphized language to describe computer operations.

This issue is not trivial, for it involves our definition of ourselves as human beings, which is somewhat uncertain at present. In fact, a new definition of "human" in 1973 betrays some problems with our human identity:

> 3b. susceptible to or representative of the sympathies and frailities of man's nature (such inconsistency is very human).

Here humanity is seen as frail and inconsistent, as opposed to the faster, stronger machinery which surrounds it.

Problems of human self-definition will only become more acute in the future, as biological "engineering" starts to produce altered DNA-based beings. This issue has been anticipated by the language, courtesy of science fiction, in the term "humanoid," first appearing in the *Collegiate Dictionary* in 1963. Likewise medicine has already given us *cyborgs* (humans linked to machines) and *bionic* body parts.

The human *identity crisis* is already traceable in current dictionary definitions. For as there has been a process of externalizing human qualities onto machines, there has also been a process of internalizing machine qualities into humans.

This internalization also goes back to the nineteenth century, when mechanistic terms started to be applied to biological phenomena (Barfield, 1985). In the 1st Edition of the *Collegiate Dictionary*, (Merriam-Webster, 1898) we find as a definition of "machine":

> 3. Figuratively, any person controlled by another's will, or a collecton of individuals working as an organized force.

The application of "machine" to humans thus had a negative connotation, which, however, is missing by 1963, when a new definition appears: "A living organism or one of its functional systems." This definition is an outgrowth of the philosophy of "mechanism," which first appeared in the *Collegiate Dictionary* in 1936 as "the doctrine that natural processes are mechanistically determined and capable of explanation by the laws of physics and chemistry." Such a philosophy is ultimately to be found behind every social science technique, for example, which insists upon rigorous statistical description of social phenomena as the only valid or "scientific" approach.

A more recent application of mechanical terms to humans is found in the term "program," which in 1983 took on the following new definitions:

> 3b. to control by or as if by a program;
> c. (1) to code in an organism's program;
> (2) to provide with a biological program (cells that have been programmed to synthesize hemoglobin);
> 4. to direct or predetermine (as thinking or behavior) completely as if by computer programming (children programmed into violence).

In addition, *9,000 Words* (Merriam-Webster, 1976) lists *deprogram*:

> to dissuade or try to dissuade from convictions usually of a religious nature often with the use of force (parents lure their children away from the communes so that he can deprogram them).

These new uses of the word "program" summarize many of the issues in the human *identity crisis*. We see mechanistic biology programming cells, unnamed forces programming children, and parents struggling to *deprogram* cult members who have lost their separate identity.

This application of mechanical terms to humans is just as momentous as the application of human terms to machines. It confuses our thinking about crucial questions. Are people machines? If so, they are clearly inferior to the faster, bigger models; and they deserve to be made obsolete. Are biological processes determined by the laws of chemistry and physics? If so, why bother giving people all those troublesome rights and freedoms, which are illusory anyway? How do you campaign for freedom for a population of mechanized automatons programmed into preordained patterns?

In discussing these issues, the language we use can crucially affect the conclusions we draw. Humans are not machines, computers cannot think. Humans and computers may resemble each other in certain respects, but they should be kept conceptually separate. If not, we may wind up granting greater rights to machines and at the same time taking them away from humans.

Pointing out a problem is frequently easier than solving it, even if a first step. But, controlling the language has been almost impossible. Perhaps all we can hope for in this situation is a widespread education into an awareness of the metaphorical nature of the anthropomorphized computer terms. If enough people are aware of the metaphorical language they use when describing computer "memories," and other terms, their thought may be less trapped by the implications of their terminology.

An important contribution of critical communication scholarship ought to be to illuminate the forms of consciousness and patterns of practice that may emerge from particular metaphors. This is not to claim that the choice of metaphors determines social practice. It is only to say that metaphorical choices have consequences in the production of coherent social life.

A change in terminology for computers may be impossible to "program," but if each person who feels strongly about this issue changes their own uses of the terms that will be a start. For the processes of langue change are anonymous and unpredictable, but must start somewhere. In this century, when so much of our reality-constructing potency seems taken away from us, we still at least have control over our own language. If we use it wisely, with full and articulate awareness of the dangers of metaphorically confusing humans and machines, we can take back some of the reality-construction process into our own control.

The Bottom Line—Are We Producing Love?

This study is being written in the late 1980s, therefore the author will use the currently fasionable expression the *bottom line*, with its accounting overtones, to designate the essential point, the crux of the matter. He will eschew the use of the *counterculture* term *nitty-gritty* for saying the same thing.

Everyone has a *bottom line*. The choice here is to put "love" on the *bottom line*. Is this a culture that is producing love?

This question may seem strange because it has not been on the agenda of serious scholarship for some time. But this was not always the case. Psychoanalysts occasionally discussed love, and the dean of American sociologists, Pitirim Sorokin, closed out a life of scholarship with a series of studies of altruism, loving people, and love itself.

Summarizing his findings in Chapter 5 of *The Basic Trends of Our Times* (1964), Sorokin noted that his studies had shown a positive link between love in a person's life and good health, longevity, and creativity. He claimed that his historical study showed that increased love in a society can pull it through catastrophes, wars, and increase its lifespan. Yet in a period of crisis, society undergoes a polarization—the good become very good, the bad become very bad. In such situations, the energy of love needs to be recognized, nurtured, and marshaled where possible into functioning social institutions.

It may seem strange to see a subheading on "The Production, Accumulation, and Distribution of Love Energy" (Sorokin, 1964, p. 194) in a sociology book. Yet, given the importance of the subject, some discussion of love in society is clearly called for.

We do not see too many new words involving "love" in our dictionaries. The *counterculture* produced *love beads* and *love-ins*, but these have largely disappeared. The only other "love" term is *lovebug*, referring to a species of fly often seen copulating along highways in the Southwestern United States.

This indicates that the culture has not been joyfully expanding its vocabulary about love. There has not been a term for saintly helpers of others, for example; although *do-gooding* appears in our period, referring to the activities of do-gooders, usually seen as meddlesome and troublesome.

Instead of terms for loving relationships, trusting communication, and social harmony, we find impersonal, technology-based terms for relationships, critical and hostile communication terms, and the general *politicization* of society into stereotyped categories.

Although adults in this period may have some distance from the new vocabulary, and choose not to participate in it to some degree, the same cannot be said for young people. For them, the vocabulary describes the world as it really is. They come to see the world in the terms they inherit, even as they use these to invent new terms. Thus the consequences of a depersonalized vocabulary will grow more severe as this language becomes more and more accepted and expanded.

While we cannot control much of the technocratic society, we do at least have control over the language we use. If we are careful to avoid depersonalizing labels for others, if we do not attribute human qualities to machines, and if we avoid *doublespeak*, we will take some of the reality-construction process back into our hands.

The language that has emerged in post-World War II America is magnificent in many respects, but it is deficient on the *bottom line* of love-production. If we avoid the depersonalizing traps in our languge, this may be our most important start to getting out of the "techno-traps" of our culture.

A vision of greater social unity is not necessarily unrealistic, considering the findings of many public opinion polls which find high degrees of agreement among Americans on many issues. For example, a series of Times-Mirror polls taken during the election year 1988, shortly after our period ends, found striking unanimity on many basic questions. Ninety percent believe government should make sure everyone has an equal opportunity to succeed. Eighty-eight percent believe in God. Seventy-seven percent think too much power is concentrated in too few large corporations, and 74 percent believe the media should be free to report any story. Sixty-eight percent think the United States has a boundless ability to solve its problems. (See *Times-Mirror*, 1988.)

Our use of language can make such social unity effective, or it can obscure whatever unity exists. We need to use our language carefully, so that we may speak to each other's common humanity, and assist in the production, accumulation, and distribution of love in our culture.

Experience, Language, and Dictionaries

Experience and Language

"Experience" was a fundamental category of the American Pragmatist philosophers of the early twentieth century (see the work of Dewey, in McDermott, 1973). Experience is the stuff of life, what happens to us combined with what we think about it, how we act, and how we are reacted to. Experience presupposes consciousness, choice, the ability to act, and the ability to learn. Ultimately, Dewey concluded, experience is a mystery. Of course it was difficult to define precisely, and almost impossible to "operationalize" for social science testing, so it has lain neglected by much social science research, despite the fact that much of that research was precisely about questions of experience.

One advantage of this study of new words is that it can illuminate questions of experience. We pay attention to certain aspects of experience. When experience changes, when new objects enter our experience, or when people start acting differently, we pay attention to these changes and talk about them. Eventually the seemingly unlimited creativity of humanity produces new words which condense and codify these new, changed aspects of experience.

New words usually build on older words and create extensions of already existing "semantic fields." These are collections of terms with similar meanings. (Some authors require a semantic field to contain terms with polar opposite meanings. I am not following this convention here.) If there have been changes in experience in a certain area, and people have paid attention to the changes and talked about them, we would expect the semantic field to expand, and/or become more finely distinguished.

New words usually start with some particular social group, with its own "discourse" within the "cultural conversation." If the cultural conversation is the sum total of talk in the culture at any given time (or over a particular period of time), then we may divide this huge mass of talk up into different discourses, which are socially situated patterns of talk. One discourse can be distinguished from another by noting characteristic patterns, vocabularies, concepts, and assumptions. People can switch discourses up to a point, and social groups are partly defined by their characteristic discourses. In this study there are words from the discourses of executives, the *counterculture*, and sexual subcultures, among others, that have entered the dictionary.

Discourses are often written down and stored in some form of "text." In this study, we have worked with a special kind of text, a dictionary. Since the sources for a dictionary are mostly other texts, we are using a text about other texts. The advantage of a text is that it allows for "reflection" upon the evanescent and changing patterns of discourses in the cultural conversation.

On one level, simply noting new words will aid our reflection on changes in our discourse. This is valuable in itself. Yet our interest goes beyond the language to what these changes can tell us about changes in our experience as a culture in the years 1961 to 1986.

Our model of the process of language change looks like this. When experience is fairly stable, then the cultural conversation tends to "fit" experience adequately for the practices of the culture, and language itself tends to become invisible, to simply be a self-evident part of the way things are. Discourses guide and interpret experience satisfactorily. Semantic fields remain relatively stable.

But when for some reason the "fit" between language and experience becomes problematic, then the language suddenly becomes quite visible, and becomes the object of increasing scrutiny. The old beliefs about the adequacy of language's representation of experience come to seem unbearably naive. Questions of epistemology ("how can we know that we know?") engulf all areas of discourse.

This has happened in the twentieth century, where both philosophy and the social sciences have taken a "linguistic turn" and become preoccupied with language, symbols, and signs (Levi, 1959). The epistemological questions have become so entangled with questions about language that a writer in the late twentieth century ventures into this area at his/her peril. Some thinkers deny that language refers, or can refer, to anything outside itself (see Jameson, 1972). In this view, language is a "prison-house" from which we can never escape into the bright light of experience.

We cannot hope to settle such arguments here. Our choice of epistemology must ultimately rest on non- or meta-epistemological grounds. We will take the position that most language does refer to something outside itself, we use it to talk about experience.

It is important to recall that this is a study of new words, which are taken to exist because they allow the cultural conversation to discuss changes in experience. There is a gap between experience and language, which these new words bridge in flashes of creativity.

To survive, a new word must be accepted into some discourse. This involves a largely anonymous process of negotiation, requiring countless speech acts by innumerable people. Perhaps this is the original democracy, where each voice is equal, although some voices are certainly louder than others.

Eventually the new word trickles into print, or the electronic media, where it is amplified through the culture and its chances of catching on are increased. (However, some words which started on this "text" level received wide circulation but did not catch on—witness Robert Heinlein's *grok* or Kurt Vonnegut's *karass*, which are in the dictionary because they are in widely read books, not because people use them in ordinary speech.)

Through all these steps a process of reflection has been occurring, sometimes appearing as an intuitive feeling that a new word is apt, or not; sometimes conscious and explicit as in the debates over the appropriateness of this or that neologism in the columns of the press.

In this model, the impetus for language change comes mainly from changes in experience, which may, in turn, be produced by all sorts of changes in the environment. In the twentieth century, the suspicion is that the primary source of change has been technological change. There is support for this view in the fact that the content analysis of the *12,000 Words* dictionary found approximately 45 percent of the new words coming from science and technology. Technology produces new "things" which need to be named, and new actions result which also need to be codified and described in the language. New "things" and new actions change experience, changing the fit between language and experience.

But technology and science are not the only sources of new words. During the 1961 to 1986 period, words from many discourses found their way into the dictionary. *Gay* terms, *soul* words, and drug terminology all contributed. New words were generated from social ferment (*hippies, straights*), education (*open classroom*), food (*corn chip*), media (*spaghetti western*), and sports (*look-in* pass).

We also do not wish to imply that language only reacts to changes. In some cases, language is *proactive*, anticipating new developments and naming them. The genre of science fiction, for example, named and described many aspects of space travel long before they occurred.

The relations between language and experience, then, are not simple. In the next section we will examine historical changes in American English in the twentieth century.

Language-Change in the Twentieth Century

Lexicographers agree that the English vocabulary has changed more in the twentieth century than at any other time in its history (Finnie and Erskine, 1971, p. 125).

Further, they point to the United States as the source of most of the change (Burchfield, 1986), and to technology and science as the cause of approximately half of the new terms (Merriam-Webster, 1986).

It is clear that nobody knows the size of the American English vocabulary with any accuracy. Nor do we know how fast it is expanding. One thing we can do is look to some dictionaries of different times, and compare them.

The expansion of American English can be clearly seen in the increased sizes of the *Webster's Collegiate Dictionaries*. These are the largest abridgements of the unabridged dictionaries, and are intended to contain the words necessary for a college education. The 1st Edition published in 1898, has 70,200 words, by the author's count. The 9th Edition, dating to 1983, has almost 160,000 words, according to the cover. This indicates that the number of words deemed necessary for a college education has increased approximately two and a quarter times over the course of the twentieth century.

We can see the interrelationship between language change and technological change in an excerpt from the Introduction to the 3rd Edition *Webster's Collegiate Dictionary*, which was published in 1916:

Within the eighteen years since the first edition of the Collegiate Dictionary was published, multitudes of scientific and technical terms have become part of everyday speech. In 1898 the automobile industry was in swaddling clothes, wireless telegraphy hardly existed outside the patent office, five years were still to elapse before the Wright brothers were to prove mechanical flight practicable. To-day words connected with all of these subjects come easily from the tongue of the man in the street, and his newspaper and magazine employ them as part of the vernacular.

Note that the radio was still seen as a telegraph without wires, and that mass media of the times are spreading the new words. Similar discussions can be found in the introductions to later editions.

Another cause of twentieth century language growth is the establishment of the industries of public relations and advertising. Earlier in the century H. L. Mencken (1967, p. 706) noted that "gag writers, newspaper columnists, and press agents" were fertile sources of new terms. The general effect of these diverse sources has probably been an increased informality in the written language, as catchy new phrases come to be valued over stodgy old reliables. Even the most respectable prints are not immune. A recent survey of "(our) most reputable, most carefully edited newspapers and magazines" found slang and informal language in all of them (Flesch, 1983). The "highest paid and most influential writers" used the most "relaxed and informal" style (Flesh, 1983, p. ix).

An example of this can be found in an article in the *New York Times Magazine* by William Safire, a columnist known for his efforts to preserve the "standards" of the language. The article, "Ten Myths About the Reagan Debacle" (1987, p. 21) contains the following:

Myth 1: The President is so far out of touch as to be out to lunch.
This view holds that Mr. Reagan's vaunted "laid back management style" actually meant that he had no idea what was going on around him.

The new term *laid back* is in quotation marks, showing some distance on the part of the author; but the similarly colloquial *out to lunch* is not.

This brings up the next point about American English. In the twentieth century, the written language has become increasingly like the spoken language.

The historian Daniel Boorstin (1973, p. 451) traces this change to technologies such as the telephone, the phonograph, and more modern storage media, which allow the voice to be extended in its range and preserved over time. While the results are usually characterized as a democratization of the language, with a breaking down of elitist distinctions, they can also be seen as a lamentable loss of standards. Here we see a massive effect of communication media on language change.

In addition, the discipline of descriptive linguistics which developed in the twentieth century further downgraded the separate and privileged status of writing. This can be seen in its basic assumptions that the spoken language is *the* language, and that linguistic correctness rests upon usage, which is relative to the situation, not absolute according to a rule (Finnie and Erskine, 1971, p. 102).

This approach allowed more terms from subcultural discourses to be accepted into the dictionary, as well as terms formerly thought of as slang or substandard. Terms from sexual and drug subcultures surfaced, as well as *minority* terms and *psychobabble*.

The issue came to a head in the furor over *Webster's Third* (1961). The editors had refused, for example, to stigmatize terms as slang, colloquial, or substandard, and drew quotations from movie stars and other media figures. To them it seemed the normal result of applying the principles of descriptive linguistics. Editors and highbrow critics were outraged, however, at what they saw as a betrayal—a refusal to uphold standards. The resulting language crisis produced a spate of books (Safire, 1980; Newman, 1974; Daniels, 1983 for example), and articles (collected in Dean, et al., 1971; Finnie and Erskine, eds., 1970).

The tension between following rules or keeping up with changing usage is inevitable, for language constantly changes but requires some rules for coherence. The argument may be endless, and in principle unresolvable. Yet most professional linguists agree with S. I. Hayakawa (1978, p. 69) that "(t)he writer of a dictionary is a historian, not a lawgiver." Still, in reaction to the debate, the American Heritage Dictionaries have been produced on other principles, with a panel of experts to recommend proper usages, and even Merriam-Webster has returned to the use of some labels.

Somewhat lost in the smoke of the battle over proper usage and labels is the fact that, as even its detractor Dwight Macdonald said, the *Webster's Third* did provide an admirable guide to current

American usage (in Dean, et al., 1971, p. 168). This quality makes it and its supplements a valuable source for the current study. The interest here lies in the "social history" of the language, rather than in defending one or another point in the debate over usage versus standards.

Perhaps it should be clarified here that this study focuses on semantic and lexical change. We are not dealing with the deeper structures of the language, what Saussure called "la langue." These change much more slowly than the vocabulary and meanings used in speech, or "la parole." Thus, the main construction form in English remains the actor-action construction (Bloch and Trager, 1941, p. 71), produced by our tendency to form sentences in the pattern Subject-Verb-Object. This S-V-O pattern, in turn, makes a substantialist view of the world seem "correct," as pointed out by Whorf (1956). We tend to speak of the world as populated by discrete things with properties that act on other things. Yet this construction is not adequate for the field theories of modern science, which posit dense regions of a field rather than discrete particles, for example (Schrecker, 1948, p. 96). Many of the problems of communicating advanced scientific and mathematical information can be traced to this linguistic difficulty. For all our change in the language, the deep structure of the Subject-Verb-Object construction has not yet been displaced.

On the level of semantics, however, the changes in American English have been enormous. How have all these new words been formed?

A study by Algeo (1980) of 1,000 words in the *Barnhart Dictionary of New English Since 1963* (1973) found that 63.9 percent of the new words were composites of existing morphemes. Thus the word *dehire* combined de- and hire into a recognizable euphemism for getting fired. Most new words build on older bases so we can recognize them without elaborate explanations.

Algeo (1980) found that 14.2 percent of his sample consisted of shifted forms, that is, older words were used grammatically in a new way. He cites the word "cool" used as a noun ("keep your cool") when originally it was an adjective. "Cool" is also cited as a verb (*cool it*) in *12,000 Words*.

Shortening of words to form new words occurred in 9.7 percent of Algeo's sample. "Jag" from jaguar, is an example.

Foreign words accounted for 6.9 percent (*macho* from Spanish, for example), and blending of words 4.8 percent (slum and suburb into *slurb*).

The great storehouse of words is, of course, the dictionary. Because a dictionary is the central source for this study, and since dictionary definitions are the units of analysis, we will take a closer look at how dictionaries are put together in the next section.

How a New Word Gets Into the Dictionary

The database for this study is a dictionary of new words, *12,000 Words* (Merriam-Webster, 1986). It was issued by Merriam-Webster to supplement its 1961 *Unabridged Dictionary*, and it contains terms felt by the editors to have become "firmly established in the language" since 1961.

The author chose this particular dictionary because he respected its predecessors, *6,000 Words* (Merriam-Webster, 1976) and *9,000 Words* (Merriam-Webster, 1983a), which are largely incorporated into it. All of these dictionaries are for general audiences, and result from a wide sampling of the language. Other dictionaries of new words are available, but did not give as representative a selection of the cultural conversation as these.

Of course the selection of new words is always somewhat *dicey*. No one can be sure which words will survive, and which will disappear, giving the whole process something of the precision of a horse race. For example, "idiot box" as a term for television was in the earlier volumes, but was dropped from *12,000 Words*, apparently because the editors felt it was no longer in circulation.

To be included in the supplements, the words must have appeared fairly widely in the sources studied by the Merriam-Webster editors. The reading programs of different lexicographers have been studied by Willinsky (1988). He reports that the periodical literature has become the most important source for new words. Scientific journals such as *Science* and *Nature* are carefully combed at Merriam-Webster, as are the *New York Times*, *Los Angeles Times*, and other metropolitan dailies to provide a more balanced national coverage. Subscriptions to various magazines are rotated, with a constant at Merriam-Webster being *TV Guide*, which also helps them monitor television programs.

Books play a smaller role than periodicals in the reading and marking program, and the editors tend to avoid fiction, drama, and poetry because these sources use words in unusual ways. This is a direct reversal of the practice of past centuries, when poets such as Dryden and Shakespeare were seen to contribute heavily to the language, and were quoted extensively in dictionaries.

Another area avoided by editors because of exotic word-use is advertising, which might explain the fact that the content analysis of *12,000 Words* found advertising terms at the bottom of the frequency list (0.13 percent of the words in the sample).

As Willinsky makes clear, it is the "polite press," epitomized by the *New York Times,* which is the most powerful influence on lexicographers. Little direct oral information is included. Dictionaries are texts that rely on other texts. Those texts usually report current discourse of only certain segments of the cultural conversation. We can expect those groups to be underrepresented in our dictionary sample that are also underrepresented in the news: minorities, women, ordinary people doing ordinary jobs, children, and the elderly.

The fact that more slang and subcultural jargon have entered the dictionary is due to the appearance of these terms in the *mainstream* press during our period. Unquestionably, the press has broadened its coverage of these groups, and the legitimacy of *Black English,* for example, is beginning to be acknowledged. A gap remains, however, between the spoken language of the cultural conversation and the contents of the dictionary.

With these cautionary notes, we may still take the dictionary of new words as a monumental effort to capture the most important ripples in the ever-changing ocean of talk. Although a social scientist might wish to have a more careful reporting of the sampling techniques, clearly the reading programs of the editors at Merriam-Webster cannot be faulted for lack of longevity or thoroughness in what they do cover.

Once a new word has been found in a number of sources over a period of time, all its uses are put together and the editors try to come up with a definition of the term. Defining is a language game in itself. Trying to fix the fluid slipperiness of some new words requires skill and sometimes produces heated debates in committees.

What the editors are doing, in effect, is dissecting discourse. A dictionary is composed of all the pieces that result. We must be cautious in generalizing from this specialized text to the experience of the culture. But if we assume that discourse is ultimately about experience, we will have a guide to the ways significant portions of the cultural conversation tried to conceptualize changed experience.

One bit of information the dictionary does not provide is a frequency count of the new words—how often they are used. The latest available frequency count for a large body of text is known as the Brown Corpus, from Brown University, and it dates from the early 1960s, before most of these new words were in wide circulation (Nelson and Kucera, 1982). Perhaps in the brave new age of computer content analysis, we will be able to quickly sample large amounts of text for frequency counts of new words. In the meantime, although these new words had to pass some minimum standard of usage, we cannot tell from our source whether *disc brake* was used more than *disco*, should we care to know.

The conclusions we can get from this study will not be final conclusions about the state of American culture, but rather hypotheses to guide further research. Since this study is unique, not having a long literature of previous similar research efforts to draw upon, it is unavoidably a pilot study. New ground is broken, but we cannot consider the task finished by this one effort.

This study falls under the rubric of "interpretive social science," as described by Geertz (1973), and will "aid us in gaining access to the conceptual world in which our subjects live. . . ." In this case, the subjects are ourselves and the conceptual world is that of our culture. We will get stories about our culture "in our own words."

Perhaps this technique does not escape the prison-house of language. But at least it opens some windows, and allows us to peer across the mysterious gap between language and experience.

The Content Analyses
of *12,000 Words*

Content analysis is a social science technique for systematically counting defined units of content of any media messages. The procedure gives reliable results when two or more coders work independently on the same data, and their results match most of the time. It gives less reliable results when only one person does the coding, yet one-person content analyses have often provided valuable pilot studies.

For this book's major content analysis of the dictionary *12,000 Words*, two coders were hired and trained in the use of a category system. Because the goal was to determine which discourses had contributed the most words to the dictionary, the categories represented different discourses: Biology & Chemistry, Sports & Fitness, Economy, and so on. After a period of testing, 47 categories were finally agreed upon. The results are listed in Table 10.

The unit of observation was the dictionary definition. For purposes of summation, each definition was called a "word" in reporting the results, since the "same" word was not really the "same" if it appeared in a different discourse with a different meaning.

The coders covered 116 randomly selected dictionary pages, out of a total of 212 pages; or 54.7 percent of all the pages. This included 4,608 major heading words, and 5,132 definitions. This means each word had an average of 1.11 definitions.

At first, the coders agreed on their codings over 80 percent of the time. As time went on, agreement went down into the upper 70 percent range. Weber (1985) has noticed a similar phenomenon, and attributes it to fatigue. The coders agreed on 78.446 percent of their codings. This produces a Scott's pi of .7733 (Scott, 1955). This is quite good intercoder agreement, considering that 47 categories were used.

The sample size was large enough to expect a margin of sampling error of approximately +/− 1.58 percent (Babbie, 1982). By splitting the sample randomly in half, and comparing halves, (the "split-half" method given in Krippendorff, 1980), the two halves correlated with each other very highly (r=.9795). These tests indicate a high degree of reliability of the content analysis, meaning that the sample accurately reflects the larger population.

Four hundred and fifty codings were double-coded. It is usually not desirable to double-code any terms, because it can throw off sum totals. However, some terms, particularly those regarding "People" and "Actions" could not be coded into just one category. The term *hacker*, for example, is both a type of person and a term from the discourse of computers. Careful track was kept of all double-coded terms.

Any content analysis faces questions of validity—does it measure what it claims to measure? In this case, the source, a dictionary of new words, was already a sampling of the cultural conversation. Merriam-Webster's *12,000 Words* was chosen over several other possible dictionaries because it was intended as a general-purpose dictionary, and relied on a large sampling of the current press. The Barnhart dictionaries concentrated too much on *upscale* journals for their sources, and Mager and Mager (1982) did not seem as reliable.

Another aspect of the question of validity revolves around the issue of just what the appearance of a definition in a dictionary means about the culture. The current study is based on the assumption that a dictionary definition means that the culture has paid attention to the word. Attention is the link between experience, as used by the Pragmatist philosophers such as Dewey and Mead, and vocabulary.

The larger content analysis, which forms the basis for the structure of the book, left unanswered some questions which posed themselves. This was particularly true in the area of communication terms, which were relatively scarce, but theoretically very important.

A second content analysis was therefore conducted, this time with only one coder, the author. The second analysis was less complicated, seeking only speech act verbs, and nouns and adjectives relating to talk. According to Wierzbicka (1986), speech act verbs are crucial reflections in the language of cultural behavior. It was felt that the information from this content analysis, although less reliable than the other, would be sufficiently important to justify its inclusion.

Although reliability cannot be measured in the traditional ways, there are indications that the one-person content analysis was fairly reliable. First, there were only two categories, relatively unambiguous, but laborious to find. Therefore error would probably consist primarily in overlooking terms, making the results conservatively biased.

Second, the author had lists of communication terms from over a year earlier, when the dictionary had been scanned for other purposes. These lists provided a check, some intra-coder reliability measure. As it happens, these lists provided nine terms additional, which had been missed, for a total of 169 terms. (The content analysis also found several terms not on the lists.)

Some internal evidence for reliability comes from the fact that very similar proportions of negative, positive, and neutral terms were found in both categories. For further details, see the discussion in Chapter 7.

We may therefore feel justified in regarding the one-person content analysis as somewhat reliable pilot study. Its main problem would be incompleteness, yet it is not probable that the proportions of positive, negative, and neutral terms would be seriously altered by the discovery of a few more terms. Since the proportions of the terms were one of the main objects of the analysis, it is highly probable that this conclusion will survive the results of a later, more thorough content analytic replication.

Table 10. *CONTENT ANALYSIS RESULTS*

Rank	*No. Words*	*Category*	*% Words*
1	695	Biology & Chemistry	12.997
2	463	Sci. & Tech Theory, Math	8.659
3	455	Other—Can't Classify	8.509
4	338	Medical, Physiology	6.321
5	254	Economy	4.750
6	224	General Tech Terms	4.189
7	219	Food	4.095
8	210	Types of People	3.927
9	209	Generic Lifestyles	3.908
10	187	Computers	3.497
11	168	Types of Action	3.141
12	154	Pharmaceuticals	2.880

Table 10. *CONTENT ANALYSIS RESULTS (cont.)*

Rank	No. Words	Category	% Words
12-tie	154	Sports	2.880
13	108	Society	2.019
14	105	Space	1.963
15	97	Politics—All Types	1.814
16	86	Drugs—Illicit	1.608
16-tie	86	Music—All Types	1.608
16-tie	86	Schools	1.608
16-tie	86	Sex	1.608
17	83	Language, Comm. Theory	1.552
18	81	Physiology—General	1.514
19	76	Automobiles	1.421
20	60	A-Bombs, Plants, Radiation	1.122
21	55	Television	1.028
22	49	Electric Power, Electronics	0.916
23	45	Psychological Theory	0.841
23-tie	45	Communication Situations	0.841
24	43	Animals	0.804
25	38	Ethnic, Minority Terms	0.710
26	37	Religion, Spirituality, Astrology	0.691
27	35	Military	0.654
28	32	Art	0.598
28-tie	32	Literature	0.598
29	30	General Media Terms	0.561
30	28	General Soc-Ec Terms	0.523
30-tie	28	Environmentalism	0.523
31	26	Movies	0.486
32	24	Records,Tapes,CD's	0.448
33	20	Journalism	0.374
34	19	Aircraft	0.355
35	17	Psychological States	0.317
36	15	Telephones	0.280
37	14	Pop Culture—General	0.261
37-tie	14	Theater	0.261
38	10	Radio	0.187
39	7	Advertising	0.130
47 TOTAL	5347		

BIBLIOGRAPHY

Adoni, H. & Mane, S. (1984). Media and the social construction of reality. *Communication research, 11,* (3), 323–340.

Aitchison, J. (1981). *Language change: progress or decay?* New York: Universe Books.

Algeo, J. (1980). Where do all the new words come from? *American Speech. 55,* (4), 264–277.

American heritage dictionary of the english language (new college edition). 1969. Boston: Houghton Mifflin.

Babbie, E. (1982). *Social research for consumers.* Belmont, CA: Wadsworth.

Babcock, C. M. (ed.) (1961). *The ordeal of american english.* Boston: Houghton Mifflin.

Bailey, C. (1975). Trying to talk in the new paradigm. In Dessaint, A. & Migliazza, E. (eds.), *Anthropology and linguistics* (pp. 79–82). Dubuque, Iowa: Kendall/Hunt.

Barfield, O. (1985). *History in english words.* West Stockbridge, MA: Lindisfarne Press.

Barnhart, C. L. (1982–86). *Barnhart dictionary companion.* Cold Spring, NY: Lexik House.

Barnhart, C. L., Steinmetz, S., Barnhart, R. (1980). *The second barnhart dictionary of new english.* Bronxville, N.Y.: Harper & Row.

Bateson, F. W. (1961). *English poetry and the english language.* New York: Russell & Russell.

Bateson, G. (1972). *Steps to an ecology of mind.* New York: Ballantine Books.

Bauer, R. A. (1969). *Second-order consequences.* Cambridge, MA: MIT Press.

Bell, D. (1973). *The coming of post-industrial society.* New York: Basic Books.

Berger, P. L. (1969). *The sacred canopy.* Garden City, NY: Doubleday & Co.

Berger, P. (1973). Identity as a problem in the sociology of knowledge. In Remmling, G. (ed.), *Towards the sociology of knowledge.* London: Routledge & Kegan Paul.

Berger, P., Berger, B., Kellner, H. (1973). *The homeless mind.* New York: Vintage Books.

Berger, P., & Luckmann, T. (1966). *The social construction of reality.* Garden City, NY: Doubleday.

Berger, P., & Pullberg, S. (1965). Reification and the sociological critique of consciousness. *History and Theory, 4,* (2), 196–211.

Bloch, B., & Trager, G. (1941). *Outline of linguistic analysis.* Baltimore: Linguistic Society of America.

Boorstin, D. (1973). *The americans, the democratic experience.* New York: Random House.

Bowles, S., Gordon, D., & Weisskopf, T. (1984). *Beyond the waste land.* Garden City, NY: Doubleday.

Brodeur, P. (1977). *The zapping of america.* New York: W. W. Norton.

Brown, R. (1965). *Social psychology.* New York: Free Press.

Burchfield, R. (1986, May 28). Interview. *CBS News.*

Burke, K. (1962). *A grammar of motives & a rhetoric of motives*. Cleveland: World Publishing.
——— . (1966). *Language as symbolic action*. Berkeley: University of California Press.
——— . (1984). *Attitudes toward history*. Berkeley: University of California Press.
Burling, R. (1970). *Man's many voices*. New York: Holt, Rinehart, & Winston.
Carey, J. W. (1975). A cultural approach to communication. *Communication, 2*, 1–22.
——— . (1981, May). *Mass media: the critical view*. Paper presented at International Communication Association, Minneapolis, MN.
Carey, J. W. & Quirk, J. (1973). The history of the future. In Gerbner, G., Gross, L., Melody, W. (eds.), *Communications technology and social policy*, (pp. 485–503). New York: Wiley.
Carothers, G., & Lacey, J. (1980). *Slanguage*. New York: Sterling.
Caso, A. L. (1980). The production of new scientific terms. *American Speech. 55*, (2), 101–111.
Comstock, G., Chaffee, S., Katzman, N., McCombs, M., & Roberts, D. (1978). *Television and human behavior*. New York: Columbia University Press.
Cox, H. (1977). *Turning east*. New York: Simon & Schuster.
Cronen, V., Johnson, K., & Lannamann, J. (1982). Paradoxes, double binds, and reflexive loops: an alternative theoretical perspective. *Family Process, 21*, 91–112.
Cross, D. W. (1979). *Word abuse*. New York: Coward, McCann, & Geoghegan, Inc.
Curtis, J. M. (1978). *Culture as polyphony*. Columbia, MO: University of Missouri Press.
Daniels, H. A. (1983). *Famous last words*. Carbondale, IL: Southern Illinois University Press.
Dean, L., Gibson, W., & Wilson, K. (eds.). (1971). *The play of language*. New York: Oxford University Press.
Del Sesto, S. L. (1986). Wasn't the future of nuclear engineering wonderful? In Corn, J. (ed.). *Imagining tomorrow*. pp. 58–76. Cambridge, MA: MIT Press.
Dichter, E. (1960). *The strategy of desire*. Garden City, NY: Doubleday.
Dillard, J. L. (1985). *Toward a social history of american english*. New York: Mouton.
Domhoff, G. W. (1983). *Who rules america now*? Englewood Cliffs, NJ: Prentice Hall.
Draper, R. (1985, Oct. 24). The golden arm. *New York Review of Books*. 46–52.
Ellul, J. (1964). *The technological society*. New York: Random House.
Estrin, H., & Mehus, D. (eds.) (1974). *The american language in the 1970s*. San Francisco: Boyd & Fraser.
Fernandez, J. W. (1977). The performance of ritual metaphors. In Sapir, J. D., & Crocker, J. (eds.), *The social use of metaphor* (pp. 100–131). PA: University of Pennsylvania Press.
——— . (1986). *Persuasions and performances*. Bloomington: University of Indiana Press.
Finnie, W., & Erskine, T. (eds). (1971). *Words on words*. New York: Random House.
Flesch, R. (1983). *Lite english*. New York: Crown Publishers.
Foster, H. (ed.) (1983). *The anti-esthetic*. Port Townsend, WA: Bay Press.
Frake, C. O. (1980). *Language and cultural description*. Stanford, CA: Stanford University Press.
Francis, W., & Kucera, H. (1982). *Frequency analysis of english usage*. Boston: Houghton Mifflin.
Fuller, R. (1981). *Critical path*. New York: St. Martin's Press.

Geertz, C. (1973). *The interpretation of cultures*. New York: Basic Books.

———. (1983). *Local knowledge*. New York: Basic Books.

Gerbner, G. (ed.). (1983). Ferment in the field. *Journal of Communication, 29*, (3), 177–196.

Gergen, K. (1973). Social psychology as history. *Journal of Personality and Social Psychology, 26*, (2), 309–320.

———. (1985). Social constructionist inquiry: context and implications. In Gergen, Kenneth, & Davis, K. (eds.). *The social construction of the person*. New York: Springer-Verlag, 3–18.

Gitlin, T. (1980). *The whole world is watching*. Berkeley: University of California Press.

Glenn, R. B., Kingsbury, S., Thundyil, Z. (eds.) (1974). *Language and culture*. Marquette, MI: Northern Michigan University Press.

Goffman, E. (1959). *The presentation of self in everyday life*. Garden City, NY: Doubleday.

Hall, E. T. (1959). *The silent language*. Garden City, NY: Doubleday.

———. (1977). *Beyond culture*. Garden City, NY: Doubleday.

Halliday, M. A. K. (1978). *Language as social semiotic*. Baltimore: University Park Press.

Handlin, O. (1963). *The Americans*. Boston: Little-Brown.

Hawkes, T. (1977). *Structuralism and semiotics*. Berkeley: University of California Press.

Hawkins, R. & Pingree, S. (1982). Television's influence on social reality. In National Institute of Mental Health. *Television and behavior, vol. 2*. Rockville, MD: National Institute of Mental Health.

Hayakawa, S. I. (1939). *Language in action*. New York: Harcourt, Brace.

———. (1971). Contexts. In Finnie, W. B. & Erskine, T. (eds.). *Words on words*. New York: Random House. pp. 68–80.

Heller, L. G. (1972). *Communicational analysis and methodology for historians*. New York, NYU Press.

Hodgson, G. (1976). *America in our time*. New York: Vintage Books.

Holsti, O. (1969). *Content analysis for the social sciences and humanities*. Reading, MA: Addison-Wesley.

Holzner, B. (1968). *Reality construction in society*. Cambridge, MA: Schenkman.

Hsau, H. (ed.). (1980). *Language and communication*. Columbia, South Carolina: Hornbeam Press.

Hymes, D. (ed.). (1964). *Language in culture and society*. New York: Harper & Row.

Jameson, F. (1972). *The prison-house of language*. Princeton, NJ: Princeton University Press.

———. (1983). Postmodernism and consumer society. In Foster, H. (ed.). *The anti-aesthetic*. Port Townsend, Washington: Bay Press, pp. 111–125.

Jeffres, L. (1986). *Mass media: processes and effects*. Prospect Heights, IL: Waveland Press.

Jones, L. (1980). *Great expectations*. New York: Coward, McCann & Geoghegan.

Katriel, T. & Phillipsen, G. (1981). "What we need is communication." *Communications Monographs, 48*, pp. 301–316.

Kellner, H. (1978). On the cognitive significance of the system of language in communication. In Luckmann, T. (ed.). *Phenomenology and sociology*. New York: Penguin Books, pp. 324–342.

Klapp, O. E. (1969). *Collective search for identity*. New York: Holt, Rinehart, & Winston.

Krippendorff, K. (1980). *Content analysis*. Beverly Hills, CA: Sage.

Lakoff, G., & Johnson, M. (1980). *Metaphors we live by*. Chicago: University of Chicago Press.

Landau, S. I. (1974). Scientific and technical entries in American dictionaries. *American Speech. 49*, (3–4), 241–245.

Landy, E. (1971). *The underground dictionary*. New York: Simon & Schuster.

Langer, S. K. (1951). *Philosophy in a new key*. New York: New American Library.

Lasch, C. (1979). *The culture of narcissism*. New York; Warner Books.

Levi, A. W. (1959). *Philosophy and the modern world*. Bloomington: Indiana University Press.

Lifton, R. J. (1971). *History and human survival*. New York: Vintage Books.

MacIntyre, A. (1981). *After virtue*. Notre Dame: University of Notre Dame Press.

Mager, N. H. & Mager, S. K. (1982). *The morrow book of new words*. New York: Quill.

Martin, B. (1981). *A sociology of contemporary culture change*. New York: St. Martin's Press.

Marx, L. (1964). *The machine in the garden*. New York: Oxford University Press.

Maurer, D. W. (1974). *The american confidence man*. Springfield, IL: Charles C. Thomas.

Maurer, D. & High, E. (1980). New words—where do they come from and where do they go? *American Speech: 55*, (3), 184–194.

McDermott, J. J. (ed.) (1973). *The philosophy of john dewey (2 vols.)*. New York: G. P. Putnam's Sons.

Meadows, D. H., Robinson, J. (1985). *The electronic oracle*. New York: John Wiley & Sons.

Mehan, H. & Wood, H. (1975). *The reality of ethnomethodology*. New York: Wiley & Sons.

Mencken, H. L. (1967). *The american language (abridged edition)*. New York: Alfred A. Knopf.

Merriam-Webster (1898). *Webster's collegiate dictionary*. (1st ed.). Springfield, MA.: Merriam.

———. (1916). *Webster's collegiate dictionary*. (3rd ed.). Springfield, MA.: Merriam.

———. (1949). *Webster's new collegiate dictionary*. (6th ed.). Springfield, MA.: Merriam.

———. (1961). *Webster's third new international dictionary, unabridged*. Springfield, MA.: Merriam.

———. (1963). *Webster's seventh new collegiate dictionary*. (7th ed.). Springfield, MA.: Merriam.

———. (1973). *Webster's new collegiate dictionary*. (8th ed.). Springfield, MA.: Merriam.

———. (1976). *6,000 Words*. Springfield, MA.: Merriam.

———. (1983a). *9,000 words*. Springfield, MA.: Merriam-Webster.

———. (1983b). *Webster's ninth new collegiate dictionary*. Springfield, MA.: Merriam-Webster.

———. (1986). *12,000 Words*. Springfield, MA.: Merriam-Webster.

Meyrowitz, J. (1985). *No sense of place*. New York: Oxford University Press.

Nelson, F. & Kucera, H. (1982). *Frequency analysis of english usage*. Boston: Houghton Mifflin Co.

Newman, E. (1975). *Strictly speaking*. New York: Warner Books.

Palermo, D. S. (1978). *Psychology of language*. Glenview, IL: Scott, Foresman, & Co.

Pearce, W. B., & Cronen, V. E. (1980). *Communication, action, and meaning*. New York: Praeger.

Phillipsen, G. (1985). Class notes, University of Massachusetts.

Popper, K. R. (1966). *The open society and its enemies* (Vol. 2). New York: Harper & Row.,

Postman, N. (1985). *Amusing ourselves to death*. New York: Viking Press.

———, Weingartner, C., & Moran, T. (eds.). (1969). *Language in America*. New York: Pegasus.

Rakow, L. F. (1986). Rethinking gender research in communication. *Journal of Communication, 36*, (4), pp. 11–26.

Riesman, D., Glazer, N., Denney, R. (1953). *The lonely crowd*. Garden City, NY: Doubleday & Co.

Robinson, J. and Converse, P. (1972). Social change reflected in the use of time. In Campbell, A. & Converse, P. (eds.). *The human meaning of social change*. New York: Russell Sage Foundation.

Rosenthal, P. (1984). *Words and values*. New York: Oxford University Press.

Safire, W. (1980). *On language*. New York: Times Books.

———. (1987, Mar. 22). Ten myths about the reagan debacle. *New York Times Magazine*, 21–30.

Scholes, R. (1980). Language, narrative, and anti-narrative. *Critical inquiry. 7*, (1), 204–212.

Schrecker, P. (1948). *Work and history*. New York: Thomas Crowell, Co.

Schumacher, E. F. (1973). *Small is beautiful*. New York: Harper & Row.

Schutz, A. (1973). *Collected papers (2 vols.)*. The Hague, Martinus Nijhoff.

Scott, W. (1955). Reliability of content analysis. *Public Opinion Quarterly: 19*, (3), 321–325.

Smith, J. (1986, Oct. 19). Naming our predicament. *San Francisco Chronicle, This World*, 5.

———. (1987, Jan. 4). A word for chicken little's warning. *San Francisco Chronicle, This World*, 5.

Sorokin, P. A. (1964). *The basic trends of our times*. New Haven, CT: College & University Press.

Spender, D. (1980). *Man made language*. London: Routledge & Kegan Paul.

Times-Mirror (Dec. 25, 1988). "The values we share." New York: *The New York Times*.

Trager, G. L. & Smith, H. L., Jr. (1957). *An outline of english structure*. Washington: American Council of Learned Societies.

Ullmann, S. (1964). *Language and style*. Oxford: Basil Blackwell.

U. S. Department of Commerce, Bureau of the Census. (1975). *Historical statistics of the United States (2 vols.)*. Washington, D.C.: U. S. Government Printing Office.

———. (1984). *Statistical abstract of the United States, 1985*. Washington, D. C.: U. S. Government Printing Office.

———. (1987). *Statistical abstract of the United States, 1988*. Washington, D.C.: U. S. Government Printing Office.

Warsh, D. (1984). *The idea of economic complexity*. New York: Viking Press.

Watzlawick, P. (ed.). (1984). *The invented reality*. New York: Norton.

Watzlawick, P., Bavelas, J., Jackson, D. (1967). *Pragmatics of human communication*. New York: Norton.

Weber, R. (1985). *Basic content analysis*. Beverly Hills, CA: Sage.

Wheelwright, P. (1962). *Metaphor and reality*. Bloomington, IN: Indiana University Press.

White, H. (1980). The value of narrativity in the representation of reality. *Critical Inquiry. 7*, (1), 5–27.

Whorf, B. (1956). *Language, thought, and reality*. Cambridge, MA: MIT Press.

Wierzbicka, A. (1986). Does language reflect culture? *Language in Society: 15*, 349–374.

Williams, R. (1983). *Keywords*. New York: Oxford University Press.

Willinsky, J. (1988). Cutting english on the bias: five lexicographers in pursuit of the new. *American Speech: 63*, (1), 44–66.

Winner, Langdon. (1977). *Autonomous technology*. Cambridge, MA: MIT Press.

———. (1986). *The whale and the reactor*. Chicago: University of Chicago Press.

Winston, B. (1986). *Misunderstanding media*. Cambridge, MA: Harvard University Press.

Wittgenstein, L. (1953). *Philosophical investigations*. Oxford: Basil Blackwell.

INDEX OF NEW WORDS